A GIFT FOR:

_____

FROM:

_____

DATE:

_____

SATURDAYS WITH BILLY

MY FRIENDSHIP WITH BILLY GRAHAM

DON WILTON

BILLY GRAHAM'S PASTOR

THOMAS NELSON

Since 1798

ISBN 978-1-4002-2397-8 (HC)
ISBN 978-1-4002-2401-2 (ebook)
ISBN 978-1-4002-2399-2 (audio)
ISBN 978-1-4041-1678-8 (custom)

Printed in the United States of America
21 22 23 24 25 BP 10 9 8 7 6 5 4 3 2 1

To Billy Graham

For to me, to live is Christ, and to die is gain.

PHILIPPIANS 1:21

Contents

Foreword

꧁ • ꧂

Dr. Charles F. Stanley

When my very dear friend, Dr. Don Wilton, called and asked me to consider writing the foreword to *Saturdays with Billy*, I immediately felt a deep sense of honor. For one thing, I have spent enough time with Don over the years to be blessed by his life, his powerful biblical preaching, and his real friendship. He has preached for me at the First Baptist Church, Atlanta, on a number of occasions, and his long ministry in Spartanburg and around the world leaves little doubt the hand of the Lord is on this man. I can understand why Dr. Billy Graham sought him out, loved his preaching ministry, developed a very close friendship with him, and wanted Don to be his personal pastor.

Don Wilton with Dr. Charles Stanley—Guest Speaker
for The Encouraging Word Advisory Council.

One of my fondest memories will always be when Don and I spent a good part of one Saturday visiting and having the best time of fellowship with Billy at his home in Montreat, North Carolina. It was a time filled with conversation, memories, Scripture reading, prayer, and encouragement.

I am also honored to write this because of my own profound love for Billy Graham. The impact of his life and testimony on my own life and ministry can never be overstated. The first time I actually saw Billy Graham preach in person was at the First Baptist Church, Dallas, Texas, in September 1954. I had a question I wanted to ask him. When I found out he was headed to the airport, my friend and I raced to the airport and arrived there just in time to talk to him. I wanted to know what he thought about being filled with the Holy Spirit. He did not know me at all. In fact, he had never even seen me before. But he turned and treated me so graciously. It was as though I was very important to him. I have never forgotten my first encounter with him. It was my first year in seminary, and it meant so much to me. When he had finished, he simply turned, walked off, and boarded his plane.

I will always remember when he came to First Baptist Church, Atlanta, to share the love of God from the pulpit for the first time. During his introduction he said something like, "Now, my friends, as I preach from God's Word today, you may hear things from me that you have all heard from Charles Stanley in this very pulpit." Of course, he was being funny, and the audience roared with laughter!

You will read similar stories about Billy Graham in *Saturdays with Billy*. Don Wilton was his close friend and pastor for many years. This book provides insights most people may not have ever heard. It is unique, and I am really excited and delighted Don has taken the time to add yet another dimension to Billy Graham's wonderful testimony for the Lord Jesus Christ.

Introduction

•ⱽⱽ • ⱽⱽ•

Just a Word

I will never fully understand why Dr. Billy Graham loved me as he did. The joy of sitting at his feet for so many years will remain deeply embedded in my heart for the rest of my life. I am forever grateful to the Lord Jesus.

Our relationship was one that grew from a personal invitation into all it became. After some ten years of friendship, Mr. Graham asked me to be his pastor. We spent hours on end just being together. This is what friends do.

Sometimes I talked and talked because he wanted me to share with him. Many times I listened and listened because he wanted to talk. Other times we said nothing. Nothing was said because nothing needed to be said between friends. We sat and ate a meal. Sometimes we took a walk, and sometimes we watched television or listened to others talking.

Saturdays with Billy, for the most part, took place on one piece of property. Mr. and Mrs. Graham's beautiful home, built on the side of a mountain overlooking a magnificent town and valley, was, for me, the ultimate place of worship.

In many ways, our times together were like worship services. Two men who loved the Lord Jesus, each with the challenges and blessings of life in his heart, sharing together and presenting their requests before God.

When we met, there were no recordings. There were no other people. Seldom were any others listening in on our conversations. He and I were free to talk, listen, share, and enjoy each other's company.

Saturdays with Billy came to me as a request from a publisher friend. This book is not a biography of God's servant. Hundreds of books about Billy Graham's life have been written. This book makes little effort to be smooth or logical or read like a novel. How could it be when it is based on memories of conversations between a pastor and his friend, sitting drinking coffee together? With the help of David Bruce, Billy Graham's executive assistant, I have done my best to fact-check the recollections of my conversations over many years. I am so grateful to David. I am also grateful to my assistant, Jimmie Davis, for her tireless work in the compilation of this project. I am most grateful to my wife, Karyn. She watched me leave our home for years, especially on Saturdays, when family time was so special. She was a constant source of encouragement as she entered into the full joy of the privilege God had afforded me. Mr. Graham loved Karyn and took great pleasure in teasing her. In his later years he even suggested to her that he come on holiday with us to the beach! How much we enjoyed the banter between us.

As God began to open my heart to make this effort to write down some of the great stories and recollections of my conversations with Billy

Graham, I met with my friend and brother in Christ, Franklin Graham. I knew I did not need his permission to write this, but I also knew that the legacy of Mr. Graham's life and testimony was to be cherished and honored. Part of my calling and responsibility in his later life was to protect his person and the vibrancy of his testimony for Jesus Christ.

Therefore, I wrote this series of episodes and stories with a number of goals in mind before the Lord Jesus. First, that the confidentiality of my long relationship with Mr. Graham would never be

Part of my calling and responsibility in Billy Graham's later life was to protect his person and the vibrancy of his testimony for Jesus Christ.

violated. Second, that everything I recalled him saying to me in conversations between two friends, at the very least, would be accurate and true. Third, that Don Wilton, pastor and friend to Mr. Graham, would not be the focus of this book by any means. I asked the Lord Jesus to allow me to be simply another instrument in God's hands. Fourth, that the vibrancy of Mr. Graham's testimony would shine through every page. It became almost impossible to write about any event, story, or conversation without repeatedly bringing up the Lord Jesus. Some might read this and find themselves thinking, *Does he not have anything else to write about other than Jesus all the time?*

Only God gets the glory, boys; only God gets the glory!

BILLY GRAHAM

Billy Graham with his dogs, Lars and China.

1

Billy's Light

※ · ※

Don't be a prude, or snobbish, but let your life glow for
Christ. We are lamps shining in the darkness.
BILLY GRAHAM

I t was as though my car just knew where we were going. The drive
was breathtakingly beautiful. Regardless of the time of the year,
the Blue Ridge Mountains insisted on beginning the conversation I
would have on that day with Billy Graham. The haze that clung to
the sides of the hills and mountains gave the appearance of smoke. As
the view came into focus, the haze seemed to roll down the hillsides
while settling peacefully on the gurgling waters of each meander-
ing river I crossed. It appeared God was speaking: "Look unto the
hills from whence comes your help. Your help comes from the Lord!"
(Psalm 121:1–2, paraphrased). In thinking back now, how many times
Mr. Graham said this to me.

The towns flashed by, and the endless stream of cars and trucks
seldom interrupted my conversation with God. Hendersonville, North
Carolina, simply ran into Biltmore and then the magnificent Billy

Graham Training Center at The Cove. It would have been unthinkable not to take the Black Mountain exit and enter into this place that lay so deeply embedded in the heart of every conversation I had with God.

Black Mountain is a quaint little town. Most days find it teeming with visitors, all soaking up the warm embrace of its lovely sidewalks, shops, and cafés. At this point my motorcar automatically seemed to know which way to go. The stone archway that welcomed all to Montreat, North Carolina, signaled an immediate left turn taking us past George Beverly Shea's home. How many times had this dear man faithfully reminded the world, "I'd rather have Jesus than anything"?

The two-mile drive up the winding road led to the entrance of the Graham home that began at the gate. This was no ordinary gate. The brief pause, followed by the swish of the card, and the wait for the inevitable and slow, but deliberate swing away from the car and toward my destiny. Seemed like this was about to be a visit to heaven. For me, at least.

The narrow but enchanting drive up to the house was wonderful. Especially the swimming pool delicately carved out between two hills at the joint. Oh! What about the little cottage that seemed to wave at me and say, "He's in!"?

It was Saturday with Billy.

The dogs often came out to offer their opinions and sidle up to my car, looking curious but somewhat disinterested. China, even though a very loving and docile Rottweiler mix, could look a little intimidating at times, but Lars, the German shepherd, although big and tough, was always available for a little charm. "Hello, Lars, and how are you today, my good fellow?" I would say. He responded by wagging his tail.

The house always looked friendly and inviting. I surveyed the parking lot and noticed which cars were there and which ones were not. Each one represented faithful servanthood of the highest order. Such amazing people, so giving, so loving—each with countless recollections of a vast world out there represented and embraced by just one man in here.

I opened the side door and entered. To my left was the comfortable sitting room. To the right, the kitchen. Yes, that warm, beautiful place in that warm, beautiful house. This was the home of Ruth and Billy Graham. This place perched on the lofty hillside overlooking forever, it would seem. This place, this retreat, this refuge, this rest, this relaxation, this quiet. Now, this world. It was as though Billy Graham's entire world could be found in the home. Nevertheless, the memories lingered of the world he knew so well out there, filled with people and places of every kind and description.

This was Saturday, and time was of no consequence between friends. Our conversation took place over a long time and was watched over This was Saturday, and time was of no consequence between friends. mostly by the dogs and the cat. Always accompanied by great food prepared by precious people, or by favorite foods delivered from restaurants "down there." Over the years, this Saturday conversation took

Billy Graham's mountaintop haven of rest.

place around the kitchen table, in the sitting room, or in the study, surrounded by books and countless pictures of family and close friends.
It also took place many times outside in the yard, sitting on favorite
chairs while sipping great cups of coffee or simply eating hot dogs
together. There the distinctive split-fence wooden railings had their
own message and conversation of wonderful times past and the calm
assurance of things to come. Those railings seemed to offer the proverbial invitation, so deeply etched into the heart of the evangelist.
The invitation to "look out unto the hills" where only the God and
Father of our Lord Jesus Christ could offer hope, joy, and forgiveness
to a lost and dying world (Psalm 121:1, paraphrased). The invitation
to "look out" to the nations and see that the "harvest truly is plentiful,
but the laborers are few" (Matthew 9:37). Mr. Graham knew it. He had

Saturdays with Billy

seen it. He heard the call of God. He had lived on that mountain for decades. This was where God spoke to him and through him times without number. This was where his soul-spirit was rekindled. This was the one place, in all of God's creation, that this one light for Jesus was ignited and set on fire. This piece of beautiful real estate was Billy Graham's haven of rest. This was where he would recharge his batteries and find solace and comfort for his weary bones. This was where the family lived that he loved so well. This was Billy's home—the home where a deep friendship was forged between two pastors. One, most certainly America's pastor, and the other just a local pastor and friend.

Despite the confines of this one location later in Billy Graham's life, every time he opened his mouth the nations were in his voice. The miles he had traveled were in his DNA, it seemed. His passion for reaching people for Christ never left his eyes. Sometimes it was just a nod. Sometimes a long explanation. Many times a question designed to provoke deep thought, offer background rationale, or simply to inquire about the God he served with all of his heart, soul, and mind. It was as if the light that shined so brightly needed to be fed a daily dose by the Holy Spirit of the living God. It was as though Billy thought he was incapable of doing anything of substance for Christ. It was as though he was pursuing nothing for himself. No fame. No glory. No recognition. No reward.

All Billy seemed to do was "look up" to the mountains to get all the help from God he could possibly muster, and then "look out" to the nations, where the people were. He could see them. He had met them. Presidents, prime ministers, kings and queens, old and young, rich and poor, famous and infamous. He wept for them. They needed to know Jesus.

The endless chatting and laughing, the digging deeper, the reminiscing, recalling, revealing, and the analyzing were really a one-way endeavor. I was simply a friend who had nothing to offer except to sit at the feet of this most precious man of God. I talked and talked but only to listen and listen. Soaking up decades of wisdom and proven integrity is impossible. There were myriads of stories, considered opinions, funny happenings, and a highly tangible sense that only God could have used this one man to touch the lives of countless people in countless nations of the world for Christ.

Jesus put it like this: "Let your light so shine before men, that they may see your good works and glorify your Father in heaven" (Matthew 5:16).

Saturdays with Billy is about an incredible light. A light that will always shine for the Lord Jesus alone.

Don Wilton visiting in Billy Graham's home.

2

Billy's Eyes

Home was a refuge for me, a place I could truly relax.
BILLY GRAHAM

Saturdays with Billy were wonderful days. He loved Saturdays. He would often find himself back home after yet another engagement. By 2005 his schedule had taken its toll on him physically, and he was ready to be home. All through that year, Mr. Graham had kept up with the demands of preaching in crusades, speaking at special events, and meeting with scores of people from every walk of life. In addition, he was writing books and articles and managing the ongoing ministries of the Billy Graham Evangelistic Association. The mandates on his time and his person were huge, and his calendar reflected it, but it never deterred his focus. The joy of his life was to share the love of Christ with the people of the world. All who met him heard about the Lord Jesus, and all who knew him understood that Jesus Christ was the Lord of Billy Graham's life.

Saturday was the time simply to be home, for the most part. I loved walking through the door and finding Mr. Graham wherever he had chosen to be at that moment. Sometimes he was in the sitting room, and sometimes he was in his study or even in his bedroom. Most often, I would find him in the kitchen. I treasured those times of fellowship around the kitchen table. While enjoying wonderful meals together we would talk back and forth about every known subject imaginable. He smiled and asked more questions than I could answer, and often, he would share the issues of life common to all human beings. I quickly learned how to evaluate his state of mind. I asked the Lord to give me a sensitivity to his inner needs as a man on mission for the Lord. Few could possibly identify with the extent of the responsibility placed on his shoulders. Perhaps just listening was sufficient. Sometimes, we were simply silent. Most of all, I could see whatever it was in his eyes.

Mr. Graham was a tall and imposing man of great distinction. He was a man who belonged to the whole world because he considered himself a humble servant of the Lord Jesus Christ. Mr. Graham was distinctively distinctive in every way. His favorite attire seemed to lean toward blue jeans, a long-sleeved casual shirt, and a light sweater. Blue appeared to be his favorite color.

"Hello, Brother Billy," I would say as I walked into the room. Yes, Brother Billy! He was so humble and so gracious—even to a young man like me. Early on in our relationship, I called him Mr. Graham. How many times he would look at me and say, "Just call me Billy, Don!"

"I cannot call you by your first name, Mr. Graham," I would argue respectfully.

"Oh, but you must just call me Billy!" he seemed to plead.

My upbringing was in full play. I would never call my elders by their first names. Besides, the love and respect I had for this man was of the highest level imaginable.

Then I looked into his eyes. Those Billy Graham eyes. So penetrating. So deep. So revealing. So kind. So humble. "I have a suggested solution, Mr. Graham," I offered one Saturday shortly after our friendship had begun to take root. "Would you allow me to call you Brother Billy?" His eyes lit up.

He looked at me and expressed his delight at the prospect. "No one, I can recall, has ever called me Brother Billy," he quipped. "At

"Would you allow me to call you Brother Billy?" His eyes lit up.

least not in the sense of the relationship we have as brothers and sisters in Christ." From that day forward this matter was settled. Always Brother Billy in private. Always Mr. Graham in public. I loved him so much.

Every Saturday those piercing eyes told a thousand stories as they gazed out across the brilliance of the mountains. His gaze shifted from the front lawn of the house, across the distant hills, and all the way to the "uttermost part of the earth" (Acts 1:8 KJV). As he sat and stared, it was as though he were back among those tribes and cultures. He could hear their languages, and he could remember the interpreters who would help him spread the message of hope. The people were his life's mission. His eyes were firmly fixed on them. "The whole world needs Jesus," he would say over and again. *There they are! The people*

Looking to the hills from Billy Graham's study.

for whom Christ Jesus died. They are like sheep without a shepherd, his eyes would cry out. He often reminded me that the Lord Jesus stood on the Mount of Olives, weeping over Jerusalem. Jesus did this alongside the garden of His ultimate betrayal and surrender. It was in this garden where our Savior cried out to the Father from the heart of His human agony. He relinquished His fear and feelings to the will of the Father. His humanity felt the agony of the cross. His divinity submitted to the will of God, the Father in heaven.

The surrender of Billy's life to Christ came through from the window of his eyes to his heart. Moreover, what was in his heart came out through his eyes, as if a shining beacon set high on a hill. It seems as though every conversation told a fresh story, and every look unveiled this man's heart from the very beginning of his journey as Christ's ambassador.

Each conversation bore witness to the abandonment of this man. He had abandoned himself to the will of God for his life. He had said yes to Jesus and had no strings attached in the carrying out of his call to serve the Lord. Jesus put it like this: "If anyone desires to come after Me, let him deny himself, and take up his cross, and follow Me" (Matthew 16:24).

Mr. Graham's eyes were windows to his soul-spirit. He could look up and an entire story would unfold. The truth came out. The messages accrued through his eyes were often direct and unequivocal. They could warn, disapprove, even chastise. Nevertheless, they could be warm and loving at the same time.

I do remember one Saturday, very early in our relationship, when the evangelist needed to get something from the study and left the room. The moment was too good to pass up. Up came the ancient video camera. I perched it on my shoulder and began to take a record of this wonderful time, which, evidently, the whole world needed to know about. I had brought the video recorder in from the car nonchalantly for such a time as this. With the two ladies—Billy's wife, Ruth, and my wife, Karyn—in my viewfinder, a sudden sensation caused me to look over my shoulder to see you-know-who arriving back from his expedition. To my dying day, I shall always thank the Lord Jesus for the very quick but interesting look I saw as those eyes seemingly suggested that this recording thing was not, let's say, in my or anyone else's best interest. Not a word was spoken, but those eyes, kind but firm, told me this was not a good idea. Never was. Never again. No! In fact, come to think about it, the first and the last ever recording I have of my conversations with Billy on any day, let alone Saturdays, is the one with "the look."

> Not a word was spoken, but those eyes, kind but firm, told me this was not a good idea. Never was. Never again. No!

For the next two decades, Saturdays with Billy were never recorded.

Very early in my relationship with him, the unsurpassed joy of being in his company was greatly enhanced by the presence of that most beloved of women, Ruth Graham. She could tell a story or two! She could laugh and tell it straight down the line. Billy loved her! In fact, he adored her, and he never stopped loving her even after she had gone to be with her Lord Jesus in heaven.

There we were one day, the four of us sitting in the living room, drinking magnificent cups of tea, the way cups of tea ought to be served. Karyn and Ruth were sipping while they nibbled gracefully on a selection of tea cookies. While the ladies enjoyed their fellowship together, Mr. Graham and I were engaged in an interesting game of sorts. Yes, right there in the house, we were enjoying ourselves by putting golf balls down the hallway from the study. Mr. Graham had even placed a cup at the end of the runway, designed to receive the rolling golf balls.

He loved golf, for sure. His extensive travel schedule and the constant crusade preaching combined with never-ending commitments to people often left him extremely tired. "I don't know how you do it," he would say in all seriousness to me. "I don't know how you get up on Monday mornings after preaching three and four times a day on Sunday. After just one sermon, in one crusade, I was finished in every way!" This was why he loved golf so much. He could get away from the crowds and relax, whether he was playing the game or watching it in the comfort of his home. You could see the sparkle in his eyes when we watched the game on television on Saturday afternoons. Besides, he knew so many of the greats and had a story about every one of them, it seemed. One of the joys I had during those years when Mr. Graham's eyesight was diminishing was watching golf on television and acting as his eyes for him. I cherish those times.

While he was on the road, a quick game of golf gave him time away with his team. They could escape together and laugh together. Even if only for nine holes. "Besides," he would say, "just think about the numerous life-lesson applications the game of golf provides: patience, discipline, practice, coordination, determination, physical fitness, team cooperation, and of course, humility!

"Nothing like a good game of golf to remind me how really useless I am," America's pastor would say as I looked at the picture of President Ronald Reagan awarding him the Presidential Medal of Freedom hanging at the end of the hallway.

Why not have a tournament putting golf balls down the passage! So we putted from time to time into the little spot at the end of the long hallway from the study. Then we would join our wives for a final cup of tea before Karyn and I headed home.

3

Billy's Home

❧ • ☙

The Bible teaches that our homes should be
hospitable and that those who come in and out of
our homes should sense the presence of God.
BILLY GRAHAM

T he front door of Billy and Ruth's home opened from the patio
and led into the beautiful living room. Extremely comfortable,
the living room oozed with a real sense of home. The piano occupied a
strategic position, allowing the pianist the opportunity not only to play
and sing but also to observe every occupant of the living room—and
even some who may be seated in the dining room. It was also adorned
with family pictures. One could only imagine the gatherings around
the piano over the years.

During the last year of Mr. Graham's life, Christian music art-
ist and songwriter Michael W. Smith stopped by the home to visit
with the evangelist. The joy of being together in that room with dear
Mr. Graham will be etched in my memory for years to come. Michael
brought great joy to Billy's heart and life and had often done so over

Don Wilton and Michael W. Smith at the Billy Graham Library
on March 2, 2018, before Mr. Graham's funeral.

the years. He sat down at the piano and led us all in the singing of some of the truly great songs and hymns of the faith. Michael played and sang "Just as I Am" before all the dignitaries who surrounded Mr. Graham's casket as he lay in honor at the Capitol Rotunda on March 1, 2018. He also sang Lenny LeBlanc and Paul Baloche's 1999 hit "Above All" at Mr. Graham's funeral on March 2, 2018.

Whether it was in his home or out on the trails behind his home, Mr. Graham loved to worship the Lord. There were so many times, over the years, when I would ask him a simple question: "What do you feel like doing today, Brother Billy?" He'd respond, "Let's talk about your sermon on Sunday," or "Why don't we pray together?" or "How about just talking to me about the Lord?" *Sounds like worship to me*, I thought.

Saturdays with Billy

Many of our conversations centered on worship. Any outside observer might well imagine a worship service was taking place in his home.

About the only thing he and I never did was sing together. In fact, we never even hummed a tune together. Most who knew Mr. Graham would heartily understand why. His personal conviction that his singing voice was not designed for public consumption had no bearing whatsoever on his profound appreciation for the value of worship in song. On the contrary, he knew Christian music was an indispensable and essential part of all of his crusades. He had an acute sense of spiritual intuition when the contemporary style of worship began to take hold of the church in America. While he never had the slightest thought of replacing his two most beloved friends, Cliff Barrows, the choir director, and George Beverly "Bev" Shea, the soloist and gospel singer, he certainly supported the introduction of contemporary Christian artists, singers, and bands into his crusades. The evangelist himself may not have preferred the louder and more demonstrative approaches to Christian worship, but he willingly embraced the future because he willingly embraced all generations. His only desire was to see people come to know the Lord Jesus Christ.

To Billy Graham the issue was Jesus. Even as we discussed the church I pastor in Spartanburg, he challenged my thinking. Our church had enjoyed a long and wonderful history of traditional worship for generations. As times began to change, we recognized the challenges associated with reaching all generations for Christ. Mr. Graham's counsel was invaluable. Long before the new wave of contemporary worship arrived in our city, the evangelist looked at me and said, "Don, what is most important to you and to your people?" I assured him it was our passion to reach all people for Christ. "Well then," he said, "lead your people to include other styles of worship. Do it lovingly but deliberately. Always be prepared to change and modify your method of reaching people without ever compromising the unchanging truth of the Word of God."

> "Always be prepared to change and modify your method of reaching people without ever compromising the unchanging truth of the Word of God."
>
> ~ Billy Graham

As I held Mr. Graham's hand, I could sense the joyful quiet of his heart on the day that Michael W. Smith came and played for us. Michael and I knelt down together, placing our hands on our dear friend as we prayed for him. It was as though the roles were reversed. Both of us had felt the gentle touch of this man of God as he would lay his hands on us and pray for us. Even when I was not physically with him, I always felt his prayers for me. Now it was our turn to pray for him in his home.

Billy's home was something special. There was an aura about it. It really did not matter through which door one entered the house. Each had a story. Each led inside. There was music in there. Many times it could be heard. Most times it could not be heard. Nevertheless, it was there.

I remember the first time I was invited to visit their home. "Can you come and see me and Ruth?" that distinctive voice inquired on my first Sunday as pastor at First Baptist Church of Spartanburg, South Carolina. This invitation was real, despite the embarrassment of having genuinely thought the voice on the phone line was someone pretending to be Billy Graham. The voice belonged only to one man. God's man. The one man who counted presidents and prime ministers, kings and queens as his friends. The same man who served and advised thirteen presidents of the most powerful country in the world, from Harry S. Truman to Barack Obama and Donald Trump. This was America's pastor, world-renowned and beloved evangelist, Dr. Billy Graham.

I was nervous, of course. It was to be expected. As I was escorted from the Montreat office up the mountain, my mind was spinning. *What does one say to such an important person? Where does one sit? How does one address someone of such high esteem?* The answer came as soon as the car pulled up to his back-door entrance. There they were. He, tall and as handsome as ever, with that distinctive Billy Graham look, dressed in blue jeans, with a blue sweater and very comfortable-looking running shoes. She—dressed so beautifully, with her hair caught back, and peering out at me through her glasses that seemed to put an accent on her lovely face and penetrating eyes. "Hello," they said in a seemingly united voice that sounded like a spiritual chorus. "Welcome to our home!"

The hand that had pointed so many to Jesus across the world opened the door for me. This was the hand that had greeted a who's who of the modern world. This same hand had been extended to audiences in most every nation imaginable. On this Saturday, it was extended in fellowship and friendship, welcoming just one more into the home where their hearts found such peace and rest. This was his castle because this was where the family was. This was where Ruth was. The place to which he could retreat, recharge, and refuel for the long journeys ahead. Like Paul did. This was his Antioch. It was his home base. It was the place where those who meant the most could gather, laugh, and eat home-cooked meals. They could enjoy the best apple pie ever made by any person on the face of the earth. This was the place where the dogs could play and retrieve every stick and every ball thrown for them to recover. This was the place the cat could curl up and nap the afternoon away. This was home! Moreover, this is where we sat, talked, walked, prayed, listened, and shared from the heart.

It did not matter to Mr. Graham who entered his home. Each person received the same hospitality. Down the line, home-style, heartfelt, genuine, and loving hospitality. Almost to a fault, really, because he was so gracious to everyone. It was common for him to tell all who came just how much he would love to see them again. Despite the obvious impracticalities presented by his most genuine invitations, it did send the staff running around the house in a state of near panic from time to time.

The challenge caused by his gracious hospitality, though, was never a problem, because he really meant it. He was no respecter of persons in any way. It did not matter to him where people came from or the color of their skin. In 1953, during the rise of the civil rights movement in America, Billy Graham felt so strongly about God's love for all people that he went into the stadium and personally tore down the ropes that separated the White section from the Black section in the Chattanooga, Tennessee, crusade. He was instrumental in promoting racial equality in many countries around the world.

The same held true in his home. It mattered not the color of their skin. It made no difference which language they spoke or what they believed. His home was the very reflection of his heart, and all people were welcomed. He believed Jesus Christ died for all people, period. All people were sinners before a holy and righteous God. "God loves you," he would say before all people everywhere. He would not preach before audiences separated by governments bent on keeping one race in subjection to another, such as South Africa's Nationalist Party, with its oppressive apartheid policy. He would not limit his handshake to the rich and famous. He would always share the love of Christ everywhere and with all people.

Billy Graham saw the whole world as "God's parish." He took Jesus' instruction to "go into all the world" literally and applied it to his own call

He would not preach before audiences separated by governments bent on keeping one race in subjection to another.

from God (Mark 16:15). He was a man on mission for Jesus Christ. His journey began right there in his home on top of that mountain in Montreat, North Carolina. Billy and Ruth Graham's home was filled with music, worship, prayer, a warm welcome, hospitality, acceptance, love, and most of all—the gospel of Jesus Christ.

The gate to the Graham homestead.

4

Billy's Gate

❧ • ☙

Jesus Christ opened heaven's door for us by His death on the cross.
BILLY GRAHAM

I grew to love driving through the gate to the Graham homestead. It always presented itself as some kind of authority. On the approach side, it suddenly seemed to appear as my motorcar automatically dropped into a lower gear because of the rather steep incline following a radical right-hand turn. In the slippery months of winter, it was common to feel the spin of the tires as the car labored up the steep slope to the gate.

This gate, however, was no ordinary gate. In appearance, it was made of wood. It did not reflect the standards of, say, the queen of England. The queen is not only a very fine lady and lives in a very fine palace, but she has a very fine gate keeping her in and the people out!

But not this gate. This gate was a message to the world, in and of itself. Symbolically, I came to view it as a door of sorts. On one side, a massive world of people searching for purpose and meaning in life. Millions of people going about their business from day to day, but doing so in the hustle and bustle of never-ending lines of traffic. The other side symbolized the central focus of the life and testimony of Billy Graham. He had the answer to what they were searching for—Jesus!

Think about this. First, the long drive to get there was a mixed bag of just about everything the world had to offer. The drive there and back became a part of the integrated journey. It caused me to think of the world Jesus had in mind when He said, "All authority has been given to Me in heaven and on earth. Go therefore and make disciples of all the nations, baptizing them in the name of the Father and of the Son and of the Holy Spirit, teaching them to observe all things that I have commanded you; and lo, I am with you always, even to the end of the age" (Matthew 28:18–20).

Just like the people of the world, I experienced every human need and feeling one could imagine. Most assuredly, I was filled with joy and expectation. What a privilege God had given to me. I experienced great joy in going to visit with Billy Graham. How many times I left my home with a song in my heart, counting the blessings of God and thanking Him over and again.

In the same way, many people in this world are filled with gratitude to the Lord for the blessings of their lives. However, traffic can also be very frustrating. The drive to Montreat, although stunning in landscape and spectacular in beauty, was arduous in traffic. None of the massive trucks that clogged the highways, even in the "fast" lanes, seemed to have any concern that I was headed to see Mr. Graham. In addition to the traffic, there were people everywhere. As cars and vehicles clogged the interstate, I could see the people for whom Jesus had died. They were young and old. Some drove expensive vehicles. Others drove vehicles that resembled seriously dilapidated containers, some of which looked like vandalized Coke machines. We all live in a vast and searching world. Until people drive up to the "gate of life," they remain in clogged traffic patterns.

The gate to Billy's home came to symbolize his genuine invitation for people to have eternal life through the Lord Jesus Christ. Billy himself was ordinary. Like the gate to his home, the evangelist consid-

The gate to Billy's home came to symbolize his genuine invitation for people to have eternal life through the Lord Jesus Christ.

ered himself as nothing of particular importance. He knew he was only made of wood. He was not grand or ornate. He was humble in spirit. He regarded himself as having no reputation, because that was what he learned from his Savior. The following Scripture represents the humble attitude of Christ Jesus.

> Let this mind be in you which was also in Christ Jesus, who, being in the form of God, did not consider it robbery to be equal with God, but made Himself of no reputation, taking the form of a bondservant, and coming in the likeness of men. And being found in appearance as a man, He humbled Himself and became obedient to the point of death, even the death of the cross. (Philippians 2:5–8)

Because of his relationship with the Lord Jesus Christ, and only through the power and presence of the Holy Spirit, Billy Graham stood in the gateway as he pointed people to life and hope. Jesus said,

> Most assuredly, I say to you, he who does not enter the sheepfold by the door, but climbs up some other way, the same is a thief and a robber. But he who enters by the door is the shepherd of the sheep. To him the doorkeeper opens, and the sheep hear his voice; and he calls his own sheep by name and leads them out. . . . I am the door. If anyone enters by Me, he will be saved, and will go in and out and find pasture. (John 10:1–3, 9)

Like John the Baptist, Mr. Graham publicly disclaimed any suggestion that he was the gate. His mission in life was to tell the whole world about the "One . . . who is mightier than I" (Mark 1:7). He told the world that there is no other door that people may enter to gain reconciliation with God. In his message titled "The Cross," the preacher said, "There is no other way of salvation except through the cross of Christ."[1] Often Billy Graham would remind people all over the world that the way of salvation was very narrow. He often quoted the following verses in his sermons. "Enter by the narrow gate: for wide is the gate, and broad is the way that leads to destruction . . . [but] narrow is the gate and difficult is the way which leads to life" (Matthew 7:13–14). He reminded me many times that if someone has taken the wrong road, it's not too late for them to turn around!

As I took hold of my card and held it to the gate's electronic device, I thought about my relationship with God through the Lord Jesus

> He reminded me many times that if someone has taken the wrong road, it's not too late for them to turn around!

Christ. I had the joy and privilege of a personal invitation by Mr. and Mrs. Graham to meet them. I, too, was nobody, really. I responded and said yes. Initially, I was escorted from the Montreat office up to the house. I met him. We talked over a period of months. He accepted me into his home. He gave me full access to his home. Over the years, our friendship deepened and became more personal and most precious. We met just the two of us more often than otherwise. We also met with many others—all of whom were his friends.

Billy Graham showed us the true meaning of the gate of Jesus. In word and in deed, the evangelist helped ease our differences and showed us a far better way. He stood between our political divides and showed us how to love one another, despite deep-seated convictions, from the Word of God. He stood as a bridge between nations that were sworn enemies. He stood as the reconciler between those who hated others because of the color of their skin or the practices of their culture.

Saturdays with Billy were, seemingly, one endless conversation about the Gate. And not the one through which so many had driven to Billy's home.

Billy saw the Gate in most everything he was and said. Times without number he wanted to talk about the Gate. His Jesus is the only Gate that could offer hope. Jesus is the only One who could give permission for anyone and everyone to gain direct access to the "top of the mountain." Everyone who gave their hearts and lives to Jesus Christ was given "the card." Just as I had a card that gave me authorization to go through Billy's gate and to his home, so it is the shed blood of Jesus by which we are reconciled to a holy and righteous God and authorized to enter His eternal presence.

In my hand, I held my guaranteed access. The gate opened in full and complete obedience to the only means by which I was granted authority to enter.

I was inside. What a beautiful place to be! Just as the beautiful mountain landscape beyond Billy's gate was a place filled with joy and sweet fellowship, heaven will be so much more magnificent than we can imagine. As Mr. Graham would say if he were here, "God loves you! Please give your heart to Jesus today!"

5

Billy's Crowds

❧ • ☙

> It is the Holy Spirit that brings about conviction of
> sin . . . repentance cannot take place unless there is a
> movement of the Holy Spirit in the heart and mind.
> **BILLY GRAHAM**

One of the things I enjoyed most about Saturdays with Billy was the absence of crowds. Needless to say! Most of the time it was just the two of us, especially in the latter years. Just two people. One, a pastor and friend; the other, a world-renowned evangelist. Millions of people had heard Mr. Graham preach the gospel of Jesus Christ in the power of the Holy Spirit. Only the Lord really knows just how many gave their hearts and lives to Jesus as a result of hearing the good news proclaimed from the heart of this one man. They came in droves to hear him. Millions of them. They were there from every walk of life. They were rich and poor, famous and infamous, tall and short, believers and unbelievers and soon-to-be believers!

Many came out of pure conviction that God was going to be there in all His mighty power. Scores came out of curiosity. So many came because a caring friend invited them. Huge investments of time were poured into every crusade by scores of dedicated volunteers. One of the most effective initiatives was Operation Andrew. This Billy Graham Evangelistic Association initiative trained believers to bring a friend to meet the Lord Jesus. Other attendees to the crusade had only heard about Billy Graham. Some had seen the advertisements on television and billboards. Billy Graham was in town! These crowds consisted of Presbyterians, Baptists, Episcopalians, Methodists, Church of God, Roman Catholics, Seventh-day Adventists, Mormons, and more. Thousands of them flocked to the stadiums and packed out the churches where this man of God was to share from the Word of the living God. Age never seemed to be of much concern either. They came and sat down, many times on hard seats made of concrete slabs. They did not seem to care about being comfortable like they did back in their own churches.

History records them coming in multitudes. Even celebrities seemed less concerned about preferential seating, and remarkably, these crowds just did not seem to be bothered by rain, wind, cold, or stifling heat. Scores of politicians were in attendance too. Many came seeking after the heart of God. Most were doing what was right and proper, but I am sure some realized the great advantage of having Billy Graham possibly endorsing their candidacy.

> Remarkably, these crowds just did not seem to be bothered by rain, wind, cold, or stifling heat.

It did not matter to Billy

Karyn Wilton and Billy Graham watching Billy Graham classics.

why they came or who they were, because he knew God's Spirit had drawn them. The message was the same: "God loves you, and you, and you!" The fact is the crowds never stopped coming his entire ministry.

On one particular Saturday, we found ourselves watching television together. This time we watched one of the Billy Graham Classics from the archive footage of his crusades. As I sat there studying the evangelist watching his own crusade, my mind wandered back to one of Mr. Graham's recorded meetings with Sir Winston Churchill. That is right! *The* Sir Winston! The British prime minister. The man with the distinctive voice and ever-present cigar protruding from his lips. The one man accredited by many for holding the British people together during their darkest hour.

Billy loved to talk about Mr. Churchill and the times they had together going back to the fifties. He shared many great memories with me about the prime minister, but this story about Billy's crowds topped them all.

The Billy Graham Evangelistic team was extremely engaged in their ministry across the United Kingdom in 1954. It was evident God was pouring His Spirit out on the team in wonderful ways. Thousands were not only attending the crusades, but many were responding to the gospel invitation to repent of their sins and accept the Lord Jesus Christ into their hearts and lives by faith. As the days and weeks progressed, one can only imagine the extent of the fatigue that began to set in. They were all feeling the long days and nights. They were exhausted, to say the least. Nevertheless, the team remained faithful in every way. Mr. Graham received countless invitations to meet with people. The demands on his time were extreme to the point that he was physically depleted.

When the telephone rang that day, Mr. Graham was inclined to turn down the invitation. Mr. Churchill's secretary, Jock Colville, was on the line. He extended an invitation to Billy to come to Number 10 Downing Street and meet with the prime minister on a somewhat urgent matter. Realizing the priority of his call to the gospel and the purpose of his mission with the crusade, Mr. Graham politely declined Sir Winston's intriguing invitation. A short time later, another call came in emphasizing the urgency of the meeting. Billy Graham received word that Mr. Churchill's personal car would be sent to carry him to Number 10 for a quick meeting together. With much laughter, Mr. Graham offered his educated guess as to why Hitler stood no chance against this compelling man regardless of the power of the Luftwaffe, the German Air Force.

The meeting took place in a small cabinet room with Mr. Graham, Sir Winston, an overwhelming fog of cigar smoke, and the repeated offer (declined repeatedly) of a glass of England's finest brandy.

> " With much laughter, Mr. Graham offered his educated guess as to why Hitler stood no chance against this compelling man regardless of the power of the Luftwaffe.

The urgency of this meeting, as it turned out, was not what the evangelist expected at all. "The crowds, Billy," Sir Winston said as he took one more puff and one more sip. "I have noticed, and my people have confirmed to me, that everywhere you go you seem to draw very large crowds." The evangelist listened intently and admitted inwardly he was rather disappointed the question was not about salvation and the hope we have in the Lord Jesus. No, it was about the crowds. What Churchill wanted to know was if Billy could teach him a few of his techniques, because, after all, "I took Britain from the very brink of disaster and saved them from the tyranny of Adolf Hitler." Evidently, Mr. Churchill lamented the fact that the size of the crowds that came to hear him speak were not nearly as large as those who came to hear Billy Graham.

In response to the pointed question, Billy shared his heart with the prime minister. He recounted his conversion and call to preach. He told Sir Winston that he was merely obeying God. He was just a simple preacher of the gospel. Jesus had changed his life and had called him to go all around the world and tell people that God loves them and that Jesus died on the cross for them. He explained that Jesus was buried, raised up from the dead, and is now seated at God's right hand in heaven. Billy Graham admitted that he only obeyed God. "God's Spirit is the one who draws the crowds," he explained to the prime minister. After some further conversation, Billy asked permission to pray with Mr. Churchill that day, and he obliged. Only God knows how Sir Winston Churchill responded in his heart to that conversation, but it was a significant day in Billy Graham's life.

When recounting the story to me, Mr. Graham pointed out that when God calls someone to ministry, it is the Lord who makes the way. The Billy Graham team prepared, advertised, and let people know they were coming and why, but God's Spirit drew the crowds.

6

Billy's Compulsion

— ❧ • ❧ —

I never go to see important people—or anyone else—without the
deep realization that I am—first and foremost—an ambassador of
the King of kings . . . I am always thinking of ways I can share Christ.

BILLY GRAHAM

Among the many valued relationships Mr. Graham enjoyed was
the relationship he and Ruth had developed with Her Majesty,
Queen Elizabeth II, and the Duke of Edinburgh. "No one in Britain has
been more cordial toward us than Her Majesty Queen Elizabeth II," he
wrote in his 1997 autobiography, *Just as I Am.*[2] Their friendship began
early in his ministry as he preached crusades in the British Isles and
continued through his life. His relationship with the royal family, and
those who came across his path because of it, provided opportunities
for Mr. Graham to share the gospel with people he never would have
met otherwise. Mr. Graham's spiritual compulsion led him to continually think of ways to share the gospel with everyone he met.

Little did I know how the Lord would use Billy Graham's friendship with the queen to help forge a friendship between Mr. and

Billy and Ruth Graham with Her Majesty, Queen Elizabeth II, after a chapel service in Sandringham in 1984.

Mrs. Graham and me. At that time, I did not realize the significance of the life lessons God would teach me in the years to come as a result of this relationship.

It all began when my good friend, Johnny Lenning, contacted me where I lived in New Orleans, Louisiana, in 1991. He was the long-time radio producer for Mr. Graham and Cliff Barrows. Johnny and I had met and become fast friends during my preaching revivals at Taylors First Baptist Church near Greenville, South Carolina. At that time, I served as associate professor of evangelistic preaching at the New Orleans Baptist Theological Seminary and traveled extensively preaching itinerantly. During those days, I had the privilege of getting to know and love Cliff Barrows, who lived on Melody Lane nearby. The radio studio was also located on his property. Johnny wanted to invite me to attend part of the Billy Graham Scotland crusades. My deep involvement in and commitment to evangelism and soul winning would benefit greatly, he thought. He suggested I attend everything I possibly could attend, including some of the follow-up that took place after each night of the crusade meetings in Scotland.

On one occasion, I attended a dinner in Edinburgh in the company of many of the team members. I enjoyed the evening—especially sitting between Bev Shea and Cliff Barrows. Laughter filled the air, and the Scottish delicacies were delicious. Sitting opposite me was none other than Sir David McNee, retired commissioner of police of the Metropolis (London) based at Scotland Yard. Sir David was serving as the chairman of the Billy Graham Scotland crusades. He was one of the most respected men in the United Kingdom. We struck up a wonderful conversation regarding my Scottish heritage and New Orleans jazz music. I told him all about my grandfather, Captain Roderick Murdo MacDonald, from Stornoway, the main town on the Isle of Lewis in the Outer Hebrides; and my grandmother, Isabella McClean, from Auchterarder near Edinburgh. We also chatted at length about the French Quarter in the Crescent City. He loved jazz and decided that a trip to the sidewalks of New Orleans sounded like a great idea. He also was intrigued with the prospect of eating beignets at Café Du Monde. Little did I realize just how important that meeting with Sir David would be for me the next day.

> "
> Little did I realize just how important that meeting with Sir David would be for me the next day.

Later that evening Johnny came to me with the exciting news that Dr. Graham had been invited to address the Scottish Parliament, an honor few foreign dignitaries had ever been afforded. Johnny pointed out to me that only a few tickets of admission were issued to members of the Billy Graham team to accompany the evangelist. "You are not one of them!" he told me with a smile on his face.

Johnny followed up my disappointment with a great suggestion. He thought I should go to the castle and simply position myself to see all the dignitaries who would come to hear Mr. Graham speak. They would be coming from all over the world, he said. It would be worth my while to stand outside the gates and watch the procession. I loved the idea.

While standing there, awestruck by the occasion, I was approached by one of Dr. Graham's top men who was on his way into the parliament to be part of the event. Around his neck hung one of those prized tickets of entry. He had access! He had the right connections! He had permission to enter.

Well, I thought, *if he can go in there, so can I—permission or no permission!*

Imagine the picture of this relatively short preacher from New Orleans walking nervously alongside a very tall Texan as, together, we passed through one security gate after another. One can only imagine just how tight the security was in a place like that and on an occasion like this. Fortunately, one security guard after another looked in our direction and observed not this diminutive American preacher with a strange-sounding Southern accent but a tall, strong, and determined man with a straight jaw and the absolute blessing of the highest authority in the land hanging around his neck! I tried to look the part, and I am certain my best American accent came to the fore with phrases like "How are ya'll doin'?"

By the time I successfully passed through all the checkpoints without being arrested and hauled off to the Tower for public execution, I was a nervous wreck. I found myself on the upper deck of the parliament building, not unlike the upper balcony in the United States Congress. I stepped down a stair or two and summarily seated myself in the most comfortable chair I believe I have ever encountered.

When I looked up, I stared in disbelief as I observed what seemed like every television camera in the world pointed in my direction from the opposite side of the upper balcony where I sat. The next minute I heard a commotion and looked around to see none other than Dr. Billy Graham and Mrs. Graham being escorted to the seats immediately in front of mine. When he sat down, he looked around at Larry to greet him and, of course, most courteously greeted me.

> " When I looked up, I stared in disbelief as I observed what seemed like every television camera in the world pointed in my direction.

When he did so, I knew immediately that he knew that I knew I was not supposed to be there. I felt like a little boy caught with his hand in the cookie jar! I smiled sheepishly and even tried to look like I was a secret service agent, there to protect and serve. Beads of sweat began to break out on my brow.

Then I heard another commotion over my right shoulder. I turned and saw a line of officials being seated in the row behind me. At the end of the row sat none other than Sir David McNee, the top cop in all of the British Empire!

Standing next to Sir David, with his hands behind his back, was the captain of the security guard of the Scottish Parliament. To this day I will never understand myself, but I just could not stop turning my head and looking at him.

Billy Graham with Her Majesty, Queen Elizabeth II, after a chapel service in Sandringham in 1984.

Finally, the captain of the guard turned to Sir David while pointing directly at me and said at the top of his voice, "Sir David, who is that man?"

Sir David looked at me. My whole life began to flash before my eyes in a desperate final act of survival. I knew that he knew that I was not supposed to be there. After all, Sir David was most likely the one who had issued the tickets.

While staring expressionless at me, Sir David thundered with great authority, "It's all right, Captain. He's with me!"

I cannot tell you the relief I experienced at that moment. A calm came over me, and my whole being seemed to unravel back into its proper perspective. I was free at last! I was lost but had now been found! I was no longer a nobody. I was a somebody!

The captain of the security left his station and came up behind me. He gently leaned over my shoulder and whispered very politely, "Excuse me, sir. I wonder if you would be so kind as to move into that section over there. The seat you are sitting in is the royal box!"

Have mercy on me! *I was sitting in the queen's chair!*

I quickly moved to the other section. There I sat and was privileged to hear Billy Graham be introduced by the presiding officer of the Scottish Parliament. This same man had been a teenager when Mr. Graham visited and preached at Kelvin Hall in Glasgow in 1955. Kelvin Hall was considered ground zero for the 1955 All Scotland Crusade. The speaker had come to accept Christ as his Savior and Lord. Now he was introducing the man who had introduced him to Christ. Again, we see the fruition of Billy's spiritual compulsion as a result of his relationship to the royal family.

The unlikely events of that day in Edinburgh taught me a number of very significant things about America's pastor. First, both Billy and Ruth had a wonderful sense of humor. They certainly approached humor from the context of their own personalities, but they enjoyed a good laugh. They barely knew me on that Saturday almost two years after the trip to Scotland. In the meantime, I had moved to Spartanburg, South Carolina, and had become the pastor at First Baptist Church, Spartanburg. After some initial visits, they invited me back to their home. I eagerly jumped into my motorcar with great

Billy Graham and Her Majesty, Queen Elizabeth II.

anticipation. There were no plans in my heart to share this embarrassing story with them that day, even though I knew at some point I would tell them because of the spiritual significance it had in my life. The sense of awe and deep respect with which I held both of them produced a sense of extreme caution in not wanting to overly project myself or talk about places I should not have been. This was certainly on top of my list.

Second, it taught me very early just how much Mr. Graham loved the Lord Jesus. His compulsion to tell others about Christ grew more evident throughout our friendship. In the ensuing years, there were times when he would just ask me to tell him this story again.

Third, and upon reflection, it will always amaze me how God

Billy's Compulsion

uses "all things" to bring about His plans for our lives. "And we know that all things work together for good to those who love God, to those who are called according to His purpose" (Romans 8:28). Even funny things!

On that Saturday with Billy and Ruth Graham, we reminisced about the crusade in Scotland. I felt in my heart it was time to share my story with them. Mr. Graham truly found the entire episode to be hilariously funny. He threw his head back and laughed out loud. He loved it. Mrs. Graham laughed as well. Then she stood up and disappeared into the kitchen. When she emerged, she was carrying two cups of tea for her husband and me. Having thanked her, I lifted the cup to my lips. As I did, I noticed the elegance of the fine china. As I took my first sip, Ruth said with a smile on her face, "Would you like me to tell you where that cup came from? The queen gave it to me!" I think I nearly bit the side of the cup in laughter!

> Ruth said with a smile on her face, "Would you like me to tell you where that cup came from? The queen gave it to me!"

After the laughter died down, the conversation quickly turned to the Lord Jesus as I shared with Mr. Graham what I learned from that day in Scotland. God showed me that, in a sense of human understanding, this is what it is going to be like when I arrive in heaven one day. God the Father is going to look at me from the throne and say at the top of His voice, "Son, who is that man with You?"

And the Son is going to say to the Father, "It's okay, Father; he's with Me!"

Just as Sir David was the only man who had the authority to give me permission to be in the Scottish Parliament that day, so we hear the Son extending His welcome, as the only begotten of the Father to all who have believed in His name. He is the only One authorized to grant us access to a holy and righteous God. Jesus is the Christ, the Son of God. Jesus Christ was completely obedient to the Father and came down to this earth. Jesus laid aside His glory so that He could pay the price for the sin of mankind. Because of this, through repentance of sin and faith in Him, we now have permission to be reconciled to God.

A number of years after that visit to Scotland, my telephone rang. On the line was Bev Shea, one of the most treasured friends I have had the pleasure of knowing. He asked me a simple question about a trip I had taken to a crusade of Billy's once: "Do you remember that incredible time you had with Billy in Scotland?"

"Yes, sir," I replied. Of course I remembered.

"I was wondering if you would mind if I included your story and a song I have written titled 'He's with Me!' in my latest book, *How Sweet the Sound*," he said. "And I have also approached Sir David. He is very happy for me to do so as well." Only the Lord knows how many people were reached with the gospel through this beautiful song as a result of Billy Graham's influence in the lives of other people.

That Saturday with Billy when I told him this story, and what the Lord had taught me as a result, I could see the compulsion in his eyes.

Billy Graham possessed a lifelong desire to share Jesus Christ in the power of the Holy Spirit, inviting all people to trust Christ as their Savior and Lord. That longing and compulsion never dwindled. In fact, it has been passed down as a spiritual legacy in many of the lives Billy Graham touched.

7

Billy's Lessons

Psalms teach us how to relate to God, and
Proverbs teach us how to relate to others.
BILLY GRAHAM

M r. Graham never seemed to quite get over the fact that the Lord Jesus Christ had come into his life. A constant theme and topic of conversation centered on the "amazing grace of God, who saved a wretch like me." I could not imagine Mr. Graham as a wretch, but he had little difficulty in seeing himself as a wretch saved only by the grace of God. Raised on a dairy farm in Charlotte, North Carolina, the young Billy lived out his early life loving baseball and doing the things teenagers do. On many occasions he and I talked about his early days. The profundity of his love for his parents matched the depth of his gratitude to the Lord Jesus for saving him at the age of fifteen. Mr. Graham loved to talk about his early years and what he had learned through his many experiences. The journey had only begun, and the young man had much to learn.

Mr. Graham seemed to engage in a perpetual effort to be pleasing to the Lord Jesus all through his life. His prayers were often punctuated with personal confession. Like all of us, he readily acknowledged being a sinner by nature and a sinner by choice. The ever-present reality of the temptations of this world was not something he only preached to others about. Billy Graham recognized his own frailty as a human being and regarded himself as the chief of sinners. He cried out to God in prayer and supplication. He believed firmly, "If we say that we have no sin, we deceive ourselves, and the truth is not in us" (1 John 1:8). He also claimed the promise of God's Word, "If we confess our sins, He is faithful and just to forgive us our sins and to cleanse us from all unrighteousness" (v. 9). He frequently talked about all the apostle Peter had to say in 2 Peter 3:14–18. To Billy, these verses were all about the need to learn and grow. It was not just the opportunity to stand and preach. The evangelist passionately believed the only way to avoid being "carried away with the error of lawless people resulting in the loss of one's own stability" was "to grow in the grace and knowledge of our Lord and Savior Jesus Christ" (vv. 17–18, paraphrased).

Mr. Graham firmly believed God uses people from every occupation to pass along lessons that, if noted and applied, would greatly enhance not only what was said and preached, but also how the message was delivered. He often explained that the quality and effectiveness of the one who stands and preaches depends largely on those lessons learned in the fabric of daily life. "Always ask yourself if God is sending you a message," he prompted. "Sometimes those messages are very important. God uses all things and is engaged in all ways to bring

Saturdays with Billy

about His divine purpose for every life" (Romans 8: 28). "You have to accept the good things and the not-so-good things that happen," he would say to me. "You have to understand that God is making and molding you to conform to His way.

"One of the greatest tragedies I see in so many people who serve the Lord today," he told me, "is that they no longer see the need to learn.

> "Always ask yourself if God is sending you a message," he prompted.

"Anyone who stops learning stops growing," he would say over and again, looking deeply through those eyes to determine if his message was sinking in.

Billy Graham was always concerned about the way he came across when relating to others. He had a God-given and profound respect for all people and was quick to learn lessons by his mistakes in dealing with them.

His relationship with President Dwight Eisenhower was a relationship that caused Billy Graham to grow in the way he dealt with people in general. Some suggested that Billy Graham's relationship with President Eisenhower turned Graham from a popular preacher to "America's pastor." The two men formed a strong partnership based essentially on friendship, mutual respect, and admiration. Together they forged quite a team in many ways. Mr. Graham recalled how they met, largely through a mutual oilman friend, Sid Richardson, in 1952. During that time, the young Billy really came to understand the significance of conversion to Christ. "If we change men," he said, "we can change the world." President Eisenhower came to admire the young preacher and sought his counsel on matters of extreme importance. After all, it was Eisenhower who welcomed the insertion of the words "under God" into the Pledge of Allegiance. He also declared "In God We Trust" as the official motto of the nation in 1956. Civil rights, racial prejudice, and oppression were significant matters to both of these men. They shared the view that racial discrimination was abhorrent in every way. In the final analysis, both played significant roles in moving the nation forward in the dismantling of racial barriers, but Mr. Graham often expressed his regret at being too slow and hesitant about it. This always bothered him and provided impetus in his later determination not to accept the pressure of governments and people to legislate and separate people based on the color of their skin. South Africa's system of apartheid was a policy of segregation and discrimination on grounds of race and skin color. Billy Graham's unapologetic stand on equality for all was evident. Graham's famous statement in 1973 in Durban, South Africa, was to over forty-five thousand people of all races: "Christianity is not a white man's religion, and don't ever let anybody tell you it is black or white. Christ belongs to all people." This adds weight to the fact that he viewed racial discrimination as objectionable as Eisenhower did.

One Saturday with Billy, the two of us were talking about the way life itself can teach us valuable lessons. We talked about several life lessons both of us had experienced. I remember sharing some regrets about my earlier ministry. He was loving and helpful as he listened and entered into my experiences with understanding. Ever the mentor to me, Mr. Graham told me about an event well documented in books and articles over the years.

Very early in his ministry he learned a lesson the hard way from his relationship with President Eisenhower. Evidently, as he recalled it, the president, who had been the former supreme commander of the Allied Forces in World War II, invited him to come to Texas to play golf.

As they were playing their round of golf, the game was on the line. There they were. Just the two of them along with the members of the security detail. Eisenhower's two terms were ending. Richard Nixon was running as a candidate for the Republican nomination for president. Just as the president was about to use his driver to hit the ball as far as he could down the fairway, the young Billy Graham asked, "Mr. President, one question I have of you." The president paused, probably not quite with the same ability as Tiger Woods when interrupted in the middle of a swing, and waited to hear this obviously important thing the young evangelist had to say. "I realize you have to be careful, but I was just wondering if you could offer just a little word of endorsement for Richard Nixon during this campaign." At this, the president put down his driving club, walked over to where Mr. Graham was standing, and said, "Billy, how many times have I sat and listened to you preach?"

"Oh, I am sure it has been a number of times, Mr. President," Mr. Graham sheepishly replied.

"Well then, Billy, can you tell me just one time I interrupted you when you were preaching?"

"Uh, no, sir, now that I think about it," was the only possible response in the face of an impending life sentence to the worst dungeon America had to offer to criminals.

"Well then, Billy, don't you ever interrupt me again when I am playing golf!"

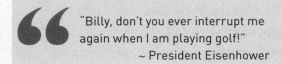

"Billy, don't you ever interrupt me again when I am playing golf!"
~ President Eisenhower

Lesson learned—there is a time and place for everything.

After Dr. Graham relayed that funny story to me, his voice softened as he recalled that tender moment a few months before President Eisenhower passed away. The former president asked his friend and confidant to tell him again how he could be sure that God had forgiven his sins. Billy Graham read the gospel verses and prayed for his ailing friend. After he prayed, the former president replied, "Thank you. I'm ready."

Lesson learned—never take the salvation of another for granted.

8

Billy's Foundation

Many times I have been driven to prayer. When I was in
Bible school, I didn't know what to do with my life. I used
to walk the streets . . . and pray, sometimes for hours at a
time. In His timing, God answered those prayers, and since
then prayer has been an essential part of my life.

BILLY GRAHAM

Many a conversation with Billy found its way back to his beginnings. "Ruth and I always wanted our home to be a spiritual foundation for our children and grandchildren," he would recall while munching on a hot dog and looking out over the front lawn of the house in Montreat, North Carolina. Even the old homestead in Charlotte, where the Billy Graham Library stands today, evokes many thoughts about this man's heart for God's work. This was the farmhouse where a foundational prayer meeting happened.

Billy's father, Frank, had joined the Christian Men's Club, a group that would often set up tents or pine "tabernacles" in Charlotte. They would invite various evangelists to come and hold protracted revival meetings in these makeshift sanctuaries. Significantly, these men gathered to pray in May 1934 in a cow pasture on the Graham homestead. That day, Charlotte businessman Vernon Patterson uttered the prayer "that out of Charlotte, God would raise up someone to preach the gospel to the ends of the earth."[3] Billy was almost sixteen at that time and had no idea that the "someone" would be him. He had no interest in spiritual things, but his heart changed after going to hear Mordecai Ham preach about six months later. It was at that meeting that he gave his life to the Lord, and that was the greatest spiritual foundation in his life.

> He had no interest in spiritual things, but his heart changed after going to hear Mordecai Ham preach about six months later.

Foundations and spiritual formations were important to Mr. Graham. He had a profound sense of responsibility to younger generations and understood the way God uses homes, places, parents, friends, and circumstances to bring about His perfect will for our lives. Mr. Graham had always said to his family that when he died, he wanted to be buried near his parents. He wanted to go home to Charlotte, where the Billy Graham Library is located. The fulfillment of his request took place on March 2, 2018. He was buried alongside his beloved wife in the Prayer Garden of the Billy Graham Library, which stands as a continual reminder of this man's humble beginnings, but most of all the legacy of spiritual foundations.

Even the casket in which his body lay was, in and of itself, a living testimony to his spiritual foundation of humility. At Franklin's request, the warden of Louisiana State Penitentiary, Burl Cain,

The opening of the Billy Graham Library. Billy Graham speaking
with the presidents in the background.

authorized the building of both Mr. and Mrs. Graham's caskets. The
names of three men were burned into the outside of Billy Graham's
casket with a simple inscription: "Handcrafted by Richard Liggett,
Paul Krolowitz, and Clifford Bowman." All three men were convicted
felons. Presidents Bush, Clinton, and Trump paid their respects, joining thousands who shed tears of joy, remembrance, and thanksgiving
to almighty God for His gift to us all.

One of the greatest foundations in Billy Graham's life was his strong
Christian family. William Franklin Graham Jr. was born November

7, 1918. His parents, Frank and Morrow, were churchgoing people who had every intention to rear their four children in the admonition of the Lord. Billy Graham commented from time to time about the cause and effect of his early rebellion, so to speak. Perhaps it was the Great Depression, perhaps not. Perhaps it was his preoccupation—thinking about girls! But then, what would a girl see in a tall, skinny farm boy anyway? He even laughed at the very thought of himself back then. Somehow he was seeing every boy for whom Christ died. Every girl. Every person. Looking back, he could see clearly. God had it all planned out.

In his autobiography, *Just as I Am*, he wrote freely about his empty heart. He spoke often to me about his random aimlessness. This was true despite loving and caring parents who read God's Word, prayed fervently, and insisted on them all going to church. Spiritual foundations to Mr. Graham were like seeds. He loved to reminisce and recall those earlier days. Looking back with a heart filled with gratitude and affection, he encouraged me never to stop sowing seeds.

Mr. Graham regarded the prayers of his mother and father, and the prayers of so many, as "the effective, fervent prayer[s]" that avail much (James 5:16). These were spiritual formations stirring and bubbling in his heart. God was preparing him to go, to see, to hear, and to respond.

In his later life, as he looked back and remembered, he was convinced these same foundations had provided some of the essential organizational values that formed the basis of the Billy Graham Evangelistic Association. The location where the gospel was to be

Saturdays with Billy

preached was but one example of this. While acknowledging that God works everywhere and anywhere, Billy Graham believed God used distinctive times and places of His choosing to reveal His glory and make His name known to people. Billy's father modeled this concept for many years. When planning for the Christian Men's Club revivals, he prioritized the selection of the evangelist, the location, and the time the event would take place. His father's determination was foundational to Billy's own ministry around the world. Billy regarded the ground upon which Mordecai Ham stood when he came to know Christ as Savior to be sacred ground in a very real way. For the majority of Billy's worldwide ministry, he would always appreciate the care given to the place they would invite people to come to hear the gospel. Nothing happened without extensive prayer and seeking the will of God. This deep commitment continues in full effect through Franklin Graham and the Billy Graham Evangelistic Association today.

Reflecting on those early days in Charlotte, the evangelist talked with great fondness of how he felt compelled to go to the Mordecai Ham revival. Notwithstanding peer pressure and family expectations, he knew the Holy Spirit was at work. The Spirit was drawing him, he declared. He felt compelled to go. The drawing of the Holy Spirit in his life was foundational to his strong belief in the work of the Holy Spirit as he delivered

> Billy regarded the ground upon which Mordecai Ham stood when he came to know Christ as Savior to be sacred ground in a very real way.

the message of the gospel around the world. He talked often about the work of the Holy Spirit when he was preaching in places and cultures where it was humanly impossible for the people to really understand all the evangelist was saying as he preached.

People needed to hear the truth, but how could they hear the truth without the "beautiful . . . feet" of those who spoke that same truth (Romans 10:15)? For Billy, Mordecai Ham was that man: called of God and fully committed to preach the Word of truth.

When Billy Graham attended the Mordecai Ham meetings, he "went forward" and surrendered his life to Christ. "Never stop inviting people to step out and come forward to receive Christ," Billy insisted often in our conversations. Jesus made it plain for us all when He said, "Whoever confesses Me before men, him I will also confess before My Father who is in heaven. But whoever denies Me before men, him I will also deny before My Father who is in heaven" (Matthew 10:32–33). This foundational truth became a hallmark of his ministry. "I want you to come," he would say across the world.

Mordecai Ham lay deep in Billy's heart all of his life. He was so grateful the Lord had sent Ham to Charlotte all those years back. He was simply God's instrument. Billy Graham was a converted man, changed by the power of the cross. God had called him. He said yes and went wherever God opened a door for him to go.

The rest is history.

9

Billy's "Just as I Am"

*Don't ever share the gift of God's love
without inviting people to come!*
BILLY GRAHAM

B y the late 1940s, Billy Graham was conducting crusades after having served for some three years with Youth for Christ. It was during those days, he admitted, he cut his teeth preaching his heart out at every occasion possible. Bev Shea, who was well received as an announcer and soloist for Moody Bible Institute's radio station, WMBI, had also joined Billy Graham. When later joined by Cliff Barrows, the three partnered together to become a formidable force for the cause of Christ across the world. One can only imagine them singing "This Little Light of Mine" in heaven together and before the throne of God. Any misconceptions Mr. Graham may have had about his own singing ability have been puffed out by the majesty and presence of the King of kings and the Lord of lords!

Let's move on to another *puff.* Despite the opportunity to lead as president of Northwestern Schools in 1947, Mr. Graham passed up the offer. It was evident the Lord was opening many doors of opportunity for the young evangelist to share the love of God in Christ Jesus with an ever-growing audience. This soon led him to Los Angeles in 1949—a time that showed itself near and dear to his heart in many conversations. Their giant tent, fondly known as the "Canvas Cathedral," was to become the single venue that propelled Billy Graham to the forefront of world evangelism. In his opinion, this was where God spoke to him and confirmed a number of critical issues. One was his firm and abiding conviction about the inerrancy and infallibility of God's Word. Friends whom he considered effective evangelists had peppered him with questions about the veracity of the Bible. Over the many years that followed, some even tried to suggest he had "altered" his stance on the inerrancy of the Scriptures. Some, like those in 1949, were close to him. However, this was far from the truth! Billy Graham always stood on the absolute truth of God's Word. It was never up to moral, societal, cultural, or even national compromise, as far as the evangelist was concerned.

> " Billy Graham always stood on the absolute truth of God's Word.

With a smile on his face, he talked freely about his "fireball" preaching and loved my summary of Charles Haddon Spurgeon's quip, "It is impossible to be about the business of preaching the Word of God and articulate snoring at the same time!"[4]

Billy Graham suggested Los Angeles taught him to trust God completely. How else could one explain the media's tendency to call his style of invitation as people "hitting the sawdust trail"? This was a throwback to that great evangelist Billy Sunday. How could the media have known that his parents had taken their five-year-old to hear Billy Sunday call on people to "hit the sawdust trail"? At the tender age of five, Billy Graham had no idea what it was all about, but he had heard Billy Sunday preach and deliver God's truth with power from God on high. The plan of God for the young boy's life was set in motion from the earliest, it would seem. His conviction concerning the public invitation may have found root at a time when his ability to comprehend was far from mature.

In Los Angeles in 1949, media mogul William Randolph Hearst ordered his media empire to "Puff Graham." That is exactly what happened—they praised Billy Graham extravagantly. As a result, the young preacher became well known overnight. Inexplicable coincidences, perhaps? "Not likely," Billy Graham insisted repeatedly. "Don't ever underestimate God's divine ability to bring to the table whomever He desires," the evangelist would quip. "Don't ever stop trusting the Lord in all things." Naturally, the conversation would morph into one of the apostle Paul's prison letters. Mr. Graham often quoted that great affirmation of faith: "And my God shall supply all your need according to His riches in glory by Christ Jesus" (Philippians 4:19).

The bottom line: he preached the Word of God in the power of the Holy Spirit and believed that God was doing His work by His Holy Spirit. His role was to "fish for Christ," which was a subject of constant conversation.

It was on the authority of God's Word the evangelist proclaimed,

"We are all sinners. All have sinned and come short of the glory of God!" he bellowed forth in that tent in Los Angeles—every night without fail. Cliff Barrows would lead in singing "Just as I Am" at every crusade, everywhere in the world. This was the bedrock of Billy Graham's "Just as I Am." His constant and persistent public invitation was firmly rooted in the Word of God.

One particular Saturday with Billy helped greatly in my understanding of his unwavering commitment to give a public invitation at the end of the sermons he preached. A friend of Mr. Graham's asked me to give the evangelist the gift of Laura Hillenbrand's book *Unbroken*. Saturday arrived, and we sat down at the kitchen table, ready to enjoy great food and fellowship together. I produced the book and handed it to Mr. Graham, saying a friend thought Mr. Graham would find its contents interesting.

"What is it?" he inquired.

"Oh, it's a book written by Laura Hillenbrand that has some stories about you in it," I answered, not knowing much about the details of the stories.

It was common for me to read to Mr. Graham. We read the newspapers and passages from the Bible all the time. His eyes and his ability to read were gradually diminishing, and so one can understand this was a blessing to Mr. Graham. Unsuspectingly, I chose several great passages from *Unbroken* and, in between bites of vegetables and meat, read away to my friend. He seemed absorbed by it all. Especially when I began to zero in on those passages that recalled how Louie Zamperini had found himself in attendance at the tent crusade in that vacant parking lot on the corner of Washington Boulevard and Hill Street in Los Angeles.

"You are not going to believe this story about a war hero who came to your crusade and met Jesus there," I enthusiastically informed Mr. Graham.

"Really?" he answered. He seemed to lean in as I read my favorite part of Zamperini's story:

"You are not going to believe this story about a war hero who came to your crusade and met Jesus there," I enthusiastically informed Mr. Graham.

Louie shone with sweat. He felt accused, cornered, and pressed by a frantic urge to flee. As Graham asked for heads to bow and eyes to close, Louie stood abruptly and rushed for the street, towing Cynthia behind him. "Nobody is leaving," said Graham. "You can leave while I'm preaching but not now. Everybody is still and quiet. Every head bowed, every eye closed." He asked the faithful to come forward.

Louie pushed passed the congregants in his row, charging for the exit. His mind was tumbling. He felt enraged, violent, on the edge of explosion. He wanted to hit someone.

As he reached the aisle, he stopped. Cynthia, the rows of bowed heads, the sawdust underfoot, the tent around him, all disappeared. A memory long beaten back, the memory from which he had run the evening before, was upon him.

Louie was on the raft. There was gentle Phil crumpled up before him, Mac's breathing skeleton, endless ocean stretching away in every direction, the sun lying over them, the cunning bodies of the sharks, waiting, circling. He was a body on a raft, dying of thirst. He felt words whisper from his swollen lips. It was a promise thrown at heaven, a promise he had not kept, a promise he had allowed himself to forget until just this instant: *If you will save me, I will serve you forever.* And then, standing under a circus tent on a clear night in downtown Los Angeles, Louie felt rain falling.

It was the last flashback he would ever have. Louie let go of Cynthia and turned toward Graham. He felt supremely alive. He began walking. "This is it," said Graham. "God has spoken to you. You come on."[5]

After listening intently as I read the entire story of Louie Zamperini accepting Christ after listening to Billy Graham preach, Mr. Graham looked at me with a sneaky smile and said, "Don, just the other day Louie Zamperini was sitting in the same chair you are sitting in right now telling me that same story!"

What?! Thank you very much, Mr. Graham! He enjoyed playfully tricking me at every opportunity. Then Billy Graham asked for a pen and proceeded to write these words inside the cover of the book: TO DON, I LOVE YOU! BILLY GRAHAM

In the shock of this precious moment I said, "But Mr. Graham, you can't give me that book. Jim gave it to you as a gift!"

"Well then," he answered, "whose book is it, then?" Of course, it was Billy Graham's book! And he gave it to me. The very gift he had been given.

With my heart nearly bursting, he reminded me of a spiritual truth that I will never forget. "This is the gospel, Don. God has given us the gift of His Son. When we receive His matchless gift, He wants us to give it to another and then another and then another!"

As I turned to head back down the mountain, Billy Graham had just one more word for me.

"By the way, Don, don't ever share the gift of God's love without inviting people to come! Just as they are! Look at Louie Zamperini." The fact that Louie gave his life to Christ following Billy

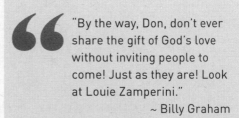

"By the way, Don, don't ever share the gift of God's love without inviting people to come! Just as they are! Look at Louie Zamperini."

~ Billy Graham

Graham's persistent public invitation left an indelible imprint on the evangelist's conviction that one should never present the gospel without inviting people to respond to Jesus.

Perhaps this helps us understand more clearly Billy's love for singing the hymn, "Just as I Am" at the conclusion of his evangelistic crusades. "Just as I Am" was much more than just a signature invitation hymn for Billy. It was one of two invitation songs that were sung the night he gave his life to Jesus Christ at the Mordecai Ham crusade. He did not go forward until every verse of two songs had been sung—"Just as I Am" and "Almost Persuaded." The first of these became the theme of his ministry and the title of his autobiography.

Just as I am, without one plea
But that Thy blood was shed for me
And that thou bid'st me come to Thee
O' Lamb of God, I come![6]

10

Billy's Face

$$\sim \!\!\! \cdot \!\!\! \sim$$

We sometimes forget that some of the loneliest people in
the world are those who are constantly in the public eye.
They have spiritual needs just like everyone else.

BILLY GRAHAM

Any person listed consistently in the world's top ranking of who's
who is guaranteed one thing: recognition. Billy Graham was no
exception. He knew it, I knew it, and the team knew it. It was reality.
Everywhere he went he carried the enormous challenge of recognition.

One of the reasons, he often said, that he loved getting out on the
golf course with his team was that he could "get away" somewhat.
Golfing became part of many of his travels across the world. Some
of those journeys were long. He and his team were away from home
and the people they loved for extended periods. Golf provided a res-
pite. It allowed this highly recognized man of God to retreat—even if
time constraints meant they could only play nine holes of golf in an
outing together. The covering of the trees and beautiful fairways provided both him and the team with temporary camouflage. He never

regarded himself as much of a golfer, except, of course, when challenging me to a putting contest down the passageway from the study to the living room. One might add I seldom backed off because of the celebrity I was playing against!

> He never regarded himself as much of a golfer, except, of course, when challenging me to a putting contest down the passageway from the study to the living room.

Daddy Bill, as his grandchildren all so affectionately called him, often recalled how he loved to teach one of his grandsons how to play the game. His grandson became quite accomplished as a golfer.

Those memories with his grandchildren were a sweet fragrance in his heart and soul all the way to his home-calling to be with Jesus. He loved his grandchildren dearly and prayed for them often.

Recognition of Billy Graham went way beyond his face. His distinctive voice had been the target of many impressionists. The first time I had a conversation with Mr. Graham on the phone, it did not take long to know who was speaking to me. At first, I thought it was someone trying to trick me, but I soon realized this indeed was the real Billy Graham. Any thought of a cute reply like, "Yeah, and I'm the pope of the Roman Catholic Church!" was quickly dismissed. No, sir! I would not dare respond to the real Billy Graham in such a manner. His voice was inextricably intertwined with his face. Behind his face was surely one of God's peerless prophets and servants.

I grew to love that distinguished face. His eyes spoke volumes without ever saying one word. Just a look could do it. His smile was sneaky in many ways and by all accounts. Seldom rapturous, seemingly controlled, always under the mantle of inner discipline—but it was there. Mr. Graham's face could question and demand, it could inquire and propose, and it could present and plead. His face had appeared on platforms all around the world and had presented, in the simplest ways, the great message of hope, love, and forgiveness, all in and through the name above every name—Jesus!

Billy Graham was well aware of his public recognition. He sure did not like it. Not one bit. One could go so far as to suggest it was

Billy Graham at his star on the Hollywood Walk of Fame.

a perpetual aggravation to him. Perhaps it was a thorn in his flesh, much like Paul's thorn turned out to be. The reason was simple: Billy Graham counted himself as nothing. He really thought of himself as the lowest person on the totem pole. He could not accommodate any thought or suggestion that he, Billy Graham, had any reason to be mentioned, seen, or considered. Even as he reminisced about being honored with a star on the Hollywood Walk of Fame, he continued to reiterate that he wanted God to be glorified and people would come to know Christ when they looked at that star.

In his later years, another visit to the Mayo Clinic for a checkup was in order. He greatly valued and appreciated the medical community. He expressed deep appreciation for the men and women who had nursed him and had taken care of him at his home and on the road. His doctors and the medical facilities had become part of his physical routine. Their counsel and constant loving care were always a topic of conversation.

This visit to the Mayo Clinic, perhaps, serves to illustrate how the evangelist received and responded to those who recognized him. During his visit, the staff had occasion to escort Mr. Graham to a balcony where he was able to enjoy a little fresh air and perhaps a good view. After a while, an unknown lady came and sat herself down right beside him. Judging by what Mr. Graham was wearing, he might have looked like a cross between the original *Godfather* figure and an FBI agent in disguise, searching for an unknown person last reported creeping around the gardens of the Mayo Clinic. On his head and pulled down low almost over his eyes was his favorite Carolina Panthers cap. To make matters more complex, he was wearing dark glasses with thick rims. Not those really nice-looking ones that cost hundreds of dollars at some fancy store. Nope, this was just a regular Walmart pair designed to do the job—hide his face!

This lady was a real chatterbox. She had a lot to talk about, especially the fact that her family back home was quite irritating, and she could not wait to get to the Mayo Clinic to get away from them. The "FBI agent" grunted every now and then.

After some time of forced fellowship, the lady looked at him and said, "You know, you sure remind me of Billy Graham," to which the face under the cap said adamantly, "I *am* Billy Graham!"

With that, the lady spluttered, coughed, and swallowed two or three times, not knowing what to do or say now that she knew! She quickly got up and left, looking back wide-eyed, all the while probably trying to determine whom she should tell first.

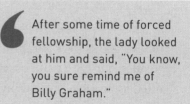

After some time of forced fellowship, the lady looked at him and said, "You know, you sure remind me of Billy Graham."

After Billy Graham officially became a member of my church, he longed to be able to come to church personally. He repeatedly expressed his desire to be part of a fellowship of people, just talking and sharing together. However, because of his instant recognition and the fear of drawing attention to himself and away from God, he chose to watch faithfully every Sunday on television. There were times he would express the desire to come to church for special services, but he was never able to attend. On occasion, and much to his great joy and pleasure, I was able to bring his Sunday school teacher and a few of our men to visit with him in his home. His teacher would open the Bible and teach us from God's Word. We would talk and fellowship and share together. This meant so very much to Mr. Graham. Even though it was not possible for him to go down the mountain to his church, mainly because people instantly recognized him, God made it possible for his church to come up the mountain to him. It would be impossible to single out any aspect of worship as being more important than another. Worship was to be Christ-centered and God-glorifying in every way, he believed.

The Lord's Supper, or Communion, occupied a very special place in the heart of the evangelist. In light of this, and because he asked me so often, I made a point of celebrating the Lord's Supper with him. As often as possible I would invite any staff present in the home to join with us. It provided a wonderful picture of the house church so clearly seen in the New Testament. From time to time I would bring one of our lay leaders from the church, or some of our ministry team. One could sense a deep presence of the Lord as, together, we would "proclaim the Lord's death till He comes" (1 Corinthians 11:26). Mr. Graham felt a great sense of obedience when he participated. He believed this was one of the Lord's commands. He also spoke of an inner sense of spiritual engagement. It was as though he was still preaching about the cross, he explained. In his later years, Mr. Graham expressed the thought that the Lord's Supper was a prime way God intended for all believers to engage in the ministry of proclamation.

A similar scenario took place over Christmas. How much he wanted to be in church. He enjoyed watching the videos I brought him of the sanctuary choir performing

The Lord's Supper, or Communion, occupied a very special place in the heart of the evangelist.

Christmas cantatas and other Christmas programs. We discussed the ministry of the choir, orchestra, and praise teams. Nevertheless, his high level of recognition prevented him from actually being there in person. His advancing age became a factor as well. Instead, I brought our ministry team to him. There we sat together, eating apple pie, laughing and sharing the wonderful Christmas story. George Beverly Shea would join us from time to time. This amazing team of servants would sit arm in arm as we shared stories, laughed together, and sang many great hymns and songs of Christmas.

Billy Graham reminded me many times, "We sometimes forget that some of the loneliest people in the world are those who are constantly in the public eye. They have spiritual needs just like everyone else." Thankfully, God can provide a way to minister to the hearts of His servants in just the way they need.

Billy Graham enjoying dinner with George Beverly Shea and Mrs. Mary Helen Wilson, widow of long-time associate, T. W. Wilson.

11

Billy's Friends

❧ • ☙

Yes, it has been a privilege to know some of the great men
and women of the latter part of this century . . . Let me stress
again, however, that most of my time has been spent with
people who will never be in the public eye and yet who are just
as important to God (and to us) as a queen or a president.
BILLY GRAHAM

Billy Graham had a special place in his heart for his friends. They warmed his heart and he spoke of them with deep and abiding affection. There were many of them. It was apparent to me that these people fell into two groups. First, just plain, down-to-earth friends. Second, all the people for whom Christ died. The former he influenced. The latter he simply cared about deeply. In both cases, he was driven by an insatiable desire to relate to them as Christ would relate to them.

The conversations we had about his friends were not only enlightening but also intriguing and heartwarming. Regardless of stature or position, most all would be drawn into the heart of this man, sometimes without realizing fully how or why—and perhaps not realizing it until much later. An aura of grace poured out of his every gesture and word. A warmth flowed from his deep-seated convictions concerning who he was in the light of who God is. Billy shared with me an abundance of personal examples. He gathered every phrase and cradled it in genuine humility, and it left no doubt as to its authenticity, especially when talking about his best friends. The men who served on his team with the Billy Graham Evangelistic Association became his lifelong friends. He cherished their friendship deeply as they shared their life and ministry together

The conversation on Saturdays with Billy was, in reality, an offering of one man's powerful presence to a friend. It never diminished with age and time. Even as his world began to close ranks and limit him more and more to the confines of his home, his presence remained strong and formidable. Words, sometimes, were a necessity, but often they were just an interruption.

> The conversation on Saturdays with Billy was, in reality, an offering of one man's powerful presence to a friend.

Billy Graham had the ability to captivate his friends. Every meeting was like an encounter with someone very special. Mr. Graham's counsel was sought after and valued. The masses of people who were unable to meet with him individually received his counsel by coming in the thousands to his crusades. His many friends made every effort to invite him to their homes and

Billy Graham, George Beverly Shea, and Cliff Barrows featured at the 60th Anniversary of The Billy Graham Evangelistic Association with Don Wilton and Franklin Graham.

offices for a personal visit. In fact, it was common for people to ask me, "Do you think you could get me in to see Billy Graham in his home?" There was not enough time in the day to accommodate all who had the desire to be with Mr. Graham. People loved and admired him all around the world.

He loved them back. He loved them all deep down in his heart. He wept for them and prayed for them. He cried out to God for them. Before I would leave for gatherings around the country myself, Mr. Graham would always ask that we pray for all who would hear the gospel. He seldom would let me leave without saying, "Please give those people my special love, and be sure to tell them I am praying for them." It was a joy and honor to tell people what Mr. Graham wanted them to know. It meant a great deal to people to hear this report. It

Billy Graham and Bev Shea enjoying a Christmas gathering with Don and Karyn Wilton.

made people feel they were his friends. Billy Graham was an extraordinary ambassador for Christ Jesus.

The thousands who flock to the Billy Graham Library in Charlotte spend hours looking at the pictures of Mr. Graham with every president of the United States from Harry Truman to Donald Trump. Every one of these men, without exception, bears testimony to their friendship with Billy. All have their own stories, some of which are public, and many of which will remain in the hearts of those so deeply touched.

In our conversations, when asked how this all happened, he simply, yet profoundly, resorted to his one-word answer: "God!" He seldom tried to explain why God allowed him to become such close friends with prime ministers, members of royal families all around the world, famous athletes, and movers and shakers. He considered it all a God thing! On the one hand he knew he had been chosen to play a unique role as God's mouthpiece; while on the other hand he could never quite understand why God would have picked him. His own unworthiness perhaps made him worthy and promoted sustained effectiveness.

When he spoke and shared, it was like listening to a heat-seeking missile. The closer he came to the invitation, the more intense and passionate the message became. God used him in a mighty way, but there was a divine contradiction happening. This same man, so confident and well known, seemed to crave real friendship. Perhaps even America's pastor needed a pastor. The greatest friends ever need great friends!

Many presidents of the United States felt the impact of Billy's friendship. They could call on him, and they could count on him. He

 When he spoke and shared, it was like listening to a heat-seeking missile.

honored their space, and the cry of their souls was safe with Billy. Mr. Graham did not try to politically persuade them one way or the other. He encouraged them to prayerfully consider what was important to them and decide accordingly. In turn this was well pleasing to the Lord our God. "Vote with your heart," he would say in conversation, "not with your pocketbook or your political affiliations." This is why these friendships were a constant theme of his life—without Republican or Democratic interference.

Most certainly, he stood strongly with platforms that honored, as closely as possible, the laws of God, but he loved the men who were in office just because they were his friends. The way he influenced them was never an exertion of himself on them. It was, rather, a gift of his presence. His keen and sharp mind carried the capacity to listen well and speak with tenderness. He never hesitated to tell the truth and always seemed to think long and hard before giving a considered opinion. On many occasions, long pauses followed questions directed at him. These were times when it was possible to think Billy had forgotten what the question was or had simply decided not to answer. Both scenarios were conceivable. However, those pauses were mostly indicators he was thinking about what he wanted to say before he answered. It was as though he was having a private consultation with God first.

Such was his influence with his friends. Most would agree that when Billy spoke, we all felt as though we were getting a word from God. It was no wonder these famous people all wanted to have an audience with Billy Graham. When they "got" him, they "got" God somehow. This is exactly what the evangelist was talking about to everyone. This lay at the heart of every message in every stadium and to all the people he loved so much. "People need the Lord!"

"God loves you," he would say around the world, but he did not limit this message to stadiums packed with people. He said the same thing to a president of the United States of America as he said to the queen of England. He would say the same thing to the king of Jordan as to the man who showed up at his house to check the plumbing. He would share this with Muhammad Ali as well as with his friend Gary Player.

Make no doubt about it: he did love being with them all. They were his friends. He loved their families and their company. He loved their homes and their palaces. He loved fishing with them in beautiful places like Kennebunkport, Maine, and he loved spending days at Camp David.

This type of friendship, perhaps, is well illustrated by a trip he and Ruth took to Washington, DC. Upon arrival, they were quite content in their hotel when the phone rang. It was the First Lady of the United States of America. The conversation may have sounded like this:

"Billy, are you and Ruth already asleep?"

"Just about."

"We are too," she said, "but we want to see you and talk. Can you come over? We will send a car in fifteen minutes to your hotel."

Billy and Ruth quickly changed into their clothes and hopped into the waiting car. Word has it the final picture of that day is delightful. President and Mrs. Ronald Reagan, in their pajamas, sitting on a balcony late at night, accompanied by Dr. and Mrs. Billy Graham, talking about their families and personal concerns.

Just four friends drinking tea together!

Mr. Graham preaching in Indianapolis, Indiana, 1980.

12

Billy's Beginnings

❧ • ❧

I have found that when I present the simple message of the gospel of
Jesus Christ with authority, quoting the very Word of God—He takes
that message and drives it supernaturally into the human heart.

BILLY GRAHAM

I t was not long after he gave his life to Christ that young Billy and
his friends T. W. and Grady Wilson began participating in a local
church revival. Mr. Graham was convinced the Lord wasted no time in
calling him into the ministry of the gospel of Jesus Christ. His "school
of learning" included a brief stop at Bob Jones University and a quick
transfer to Florida Bible Institute. "God had a plan for me," he said,
"even though I was not fully aware of the plan at the time!" As far as
the evangelist was concerned, those who were "called according to His
purpose" were simply in the hands of a loving God (Romans 8:28).
Billy considered his early life and humble beginnings to be significant
in the shaping of his life and testimony. The series of happenings that
led him to realize the extent of God's call in his life remained with him
all the way through his life.

On many occasions he would remark, "You cannot make these things up." Perhaps few happenings were dearer to him than his time in Florida. John Minder, the school's dean, invited the youthful Billy Graham to accompany him to a conference center. The pastor responsible for the meeting had asked Minder to preach one Sunday evening at his church, but Minder had a better idea. He would ask Billy to preach. Without much knowledge and certainly in fear and trembling, Billy Graham did just that! He added, "Glad they didn't have recordings of those messages—I am not sure if I knew what I was saying or where I was in the Bible!"

This early beginning was the very time at which God spoke to the heart of Billy Graham. He fought and wrestled with the call of God for over a year. Finally, he yielded to the voice of the Lord. Facedown on a golf course, he cried out, "O God, if You want me to serve You, I will!" It was 1938, and Billy Graham was barely twenty. Later he wrote these words in his autobiography: "From that night in 1938 on, my purpose and objectives in life were set. I knew that I would be a preacher of the Gospel."[7]

God still had a lot of training for him to go through. There was his time at Wheaton College and his accompanying endeavors as pastor of the United Gospel Tabernacle, which was started by students of Wheaton in a nearby lodge—as well as his ministry (with Ruth) as pastor of the Western Springs Baptist Church in Western Springs, Illinois.

No one could match the significance of his beautiful Ruth. Having grown up in China as the daughter of Dr. and Mrs. L. Nelson Bell,

Ruth was "the most precious gift" God could ever have given to Billy. He loved her and cherished their life together. Despite her desire for them to go to Tibet as missionaries, she knew that God was calling her husband to the world. Her life and influence could never be overstated, and she never left his heart.

Saturdays with Billy often involved conversations about early experiences that, he believed, were purposefully designed by God to put His imprint on Billy's heart. They helped formulate some of his personal habits and disciplines, and they included people who would embark on this extraordinary journey with him.

Ruth was the most significant of all. One time Mr. Graham was somewhere deep in a South American jungle where many people needed to hear that God loved them and Jesus died for them on a cross. News took a while to travel to those remote parts, but when word from the United States came, it was not good at all. Ruth had broken her back while playing with the children. The love of his life was stricken, and he was in the jungle, far from her. He finally was able to make some kind of radio contact and was quick to let the family know he would be home as soon as possible. The reply was quick and to the point. "Billy, there are too many people in that part of the world who need Jesus. All I have done is broken my back. You stay right where you are!"

In 2016 Billy Graham, Bev

> Ruth had broken her back while playing with the children. The love of his life was stricken, and he was in the jungle, far from her.

Shea, and Cliff Barrows sat on the stage at the Billy Graham Library, perhaps for the last time. It was a truly wonderful evening. After singing "This Little Light of Mine," Cliff asked his longtime friend, "Bill, if you had one more choice in your life, what would you like to do?" Mr. Graham pondered the question and then said to all gathered, "See Ruth! She was the most wonderful woman that ever lived, as far as I am concerned. She walked with God; she loved the Lord with all her heart. She had three or four Bibles and wrote detailed notes in all of them. She lived for the Lord, and her children would testify she taught them what it means to follow Christ." God had called Ruth, and she served Him faithfully alongside Billy until He called her home on June 14, 2007.

Even when Ruth was gone, Billy Graham's call from God never left him. From the beginning, the fear he experienced when asked to preach his first sermon at the beginning never left him. The friends he made at the beginning never left him. The lessons he learned in the local church and the love he had for the work of the local church never left him. The home they built on the mountain and the longing to be at home with his family never left him. The passionate desire to tell people about Jesus Christ never left him. The love he had for Ruth never left him.

"Tell those young preachers," he would say, "to start right and make every minute count. If you start right with the Lord, you will finish right with the Lord."

Don Wilton praying for Billy Graham at the 60th anniversary of the Billy Graham Evangelistic Association.

On one Saturday with Billy, I asked him a question. "Brother Billy," I asked, "please tell me what I need to know as I try to serve the Lord!"

He looked at me for the longest time, and then he began to talk.

"Go back to your beginnings with God. God will never be able to use you unless you are totally surrendered to Him. A surrendered man never forgets where he came from as a sinner separated from Christ. From a heart of gratitude will flow loving the Lord with all your heart and soul and mind. From the act of surrender will come the love you have for your wife and your children. From that same heart will flow the love with which you love your people and preach the Word. It will keep you on your knees. Do not ever forget where you came from. Do not ever forget your nerves. Do not ever get too big or too important. Walk away from positions, and seek only to please the Lord."

Then he put it all into the right perspective.

"You cannot serve the Lord Jesus and be alive to yourself at the same time."

Taking me to Paul's dramatic declaration, Mr. Graham quoted, "I have been crucified with Christ; it is no longer I who live, but Christ lives in me; and the life which I now live in the flesh I live by faith in the Son of God, who loved me and gave Himself for me" (Galatians 2:20).

"Always go back to your beginnings, above all with God. See yourself there at the foot of the cross," he said.

With this, Mr. Graham placed both of his hands on my head and he prayed for me.

It was at that very moment I realized I could never explain Billy Graham. Only God could. "God resists the proud, but gives grace to the humble" (James 4:6).

Little did I know that on March 2, 2018, I would have the privilege of quoting this same verse at his graveside service, in an effort to explain this humble servant of the Lord to a listening world.

13

Billy's Humor

---❧ • ☙---

What I find disturbing in America is the consuming
desire for leisure, convenience, and fun.
It seems we, as a nation, have traded God for gadgets.

BILLY GRAHAM

Billy's humor is an unlikely subject for sure, for no real reason except Billy Graham was not known for being funny. It was not that he was austere or perpetually serious. It most certainly was not because he was grumpy. Those closest to him probably have more humorous stories about him than one could possibly imagine. Often, he was funny without intending to be.

The truth is he was a serious man, even on Saturdays. His serious-mindedness came with his persona. God designed his personality to be serious. It came from his soul-spirit. Do not confuse *serious* with *unhappy*. Certainly, he was seldom unhappy—except when his coffee had to be thickened according to the way his doctor wanted it!

Serious was the way God made this amazing man. Most of his friends knew that any time spent with him would be time well spent.

He was serious about his conversation. He made the most of his words. It was not a laughing matter. It was a joyful thing, but salvation was critical because, without it, there would be no possibility of going to heaven. Hell was a reality to Billy. It was not a figure of speech. It was as Jesus had said when He told the story about the rich man and Lazarus in Luke 16. These two men both lived on this earth. Jesus said so. Jesus had no reason to summon one of His angels to help Him concoct some story about two so-called men living a so-called life and suffering a so-called death to go to a so-called heaven and to a so-called hell. No. Jesus said they both lived, and they both died. The one who had a personal relationship with Jesus went to heaven. The one who did not have a personal relationship with Jesus went to hell. In addition, Jesus did not stop there at the point of death. He went on to explain in elaborate details the suffering of the once-rich man in eternal hell. The ability to think about his sin. The ability to see all of the suffering. The ability to know and recognize that it will continue for eternity. The ability to beg for water and be denied. The cry of his heart. The agonizing separation from his loved ones. The final desperate plea to send someone back from the grave because he realized death was final.

There was nothing humorous about what Jesus said here. People all around the world were dying and going to hell. Mr. Graham was constrained by the love of God to share Jesus' saving message of hope and joy with our lost and dying world. He was God's ambassador, and he took this responsibility seriously.

Billy Graham punctuated his sermons with illustrations about

Saturdays with Billy

people and the world in which they found themselves. It was imperative for the evangelist to connect with his audience—to acquaint himself fully with the people to whom he was preaching. He strove to know as much about them and their culture as possible. This was very serious business. Even his sermons had very few hilarious illustrations, and when he did use humor, it sometimes was greeted with polite laughter, perhaps not unlike the polite laughter that accompanied his efforts to sing. Besides this, he strongly believed that illustrations were designed to illustrate the truth of God's Word. Funny stories that had

The day I stole Billy Graham's yogurt.

little end except themselves were of no value to a sermon. However, his sense of humor took on a new flavor in his later years.

After Dr. Graham's health prevented him from traveling and preaching, our time together increasingly developed into opportunities to bring a smile to his face. "Growing older is not for sissies," he concurred. Heading home to heaven could be very challenging, but with the absence of crowds, he could smile more without the serious business of preaching the gospel. Just two friends having a good time together.

Dining was simple. Just a round, well-used family table with a wooden lazy Susan in the middle, designed to turn at the mere shift of the finger of the one who needed some more of that delicious potato salad. This was the scene of many great times of eating and fellowship. Especially the ribs from Twelve Bones down the road near Asheville.

Then there was the yogurt. Billy thoroughly enjoyed his yogurt. "Have some of mine," he said with a gallant gesture one Saturday.

Certainly one to oblige, I did. "Have some more," he said again. Obviously wanting to please him, I did again, again, and again. At this point, the one who owned the bowl of yogurt to begin with leaned forward and pushed the button. This was the button perched close to his hand for easy access to a most precious group of people. The response was immediate. "Yes, Mr. Graham. May I help you in any way?"

"Please, Amy, would you mind getting me some more yogurt?" As soon as she opened the refrigerator door, he quietly added, "And get Don some of his own yogurt while you are there. He has stolen all of mine!" Not many have had the joy of being accused of stealing yogurt from America's pastor!

As the world began to close ranks on Mr. Graham, the memories of countless trips down the mountain weighed in on him. There were the shops, the restaurants, the family outings, and the people for whom Christ had died. The longing for the past overwhelmed Mr. Graham one particular Saturday. Even a world-renowned evangelist can plot his own escape. Not that he felt unloved or uncared for! Not in the least. On the contrary; his gratitude grew with each passing month and year. He was particularly grateful to those who took such great care of the house and the gardens. He so much loved the medical community who tirelessly and tenderly cared for his every need. He profoundly appreciated the consistent loyalty of his closest executive assistant, David Bruce, who was at his side perpetually. How much he loved and was grateful for his board of directors, family members, and friends all over the world.

That did not stop him from conjuring up an adventurous breakout and trying to draft me to help him do it.

 Even a world-renowned evangelist can plot his own escape.

Talk about a predicament! What would you say to such a one as this man? How could anyone possibly turn him down? Perpetual banishment comes to mind. Public humiliation, perhaps even public ridicule to the one who looked Billy Graham in the face and denied a simple request. It happened only one time. He was sprightly that day as I threw a few sticks for China and Sam to retrieve. He loved those dogs! Just watching them run back and forth across the lawn brought a smile to his face.

"Don," he said.

"Yes, Brother Billy," I called, ready to spring into action at his request.

"Why don't you sneak me out of the house today?" he said as he leaned in toward me.

What did I just hear? "You mean, like put you in the back of my motorcar and drive you down the mountain?"

"Yes," he answered. "I just feel like going to McDonald's in Black Mountain and getting a real hamburger."

What was I hearing? "You want fries with that, Brother Billy?"

Oh yes, he did. "Enough of this doctor stuff," he said with a slight grin on his face. "Can't eat this, and can't eat that. I'm ready for some real food!"

"Can't eat this, and can't eat that. I'm ready for some real food!"
~ Billy Graham

For just a minute, I thought Billy Graham was serious. One look told me he well might have been. Of course, I developed an elaborate escape plan that included putting him in the trunk of the car so the security cameras would not be able to see him. In all honesty, God was also giving me a very clear vision of myself

Saturdays with Billy

sitting in the local jail. I could see the headlines in newspapers across the world:

Billy Graham's Pastor and Friend Caught Red-Handed by David Bruce, Dr. Graham's Chief Guardian, While Sneaking the Evangelist Down the Hill to Get Contraband Food at McDonald's in Violation of Doctor's Orders!

What a cherished time, as Mr. Graham and I laughed our heads off that day as we finished off our healthy lunch right there in his kitchen.

14

Billy's Regrets

❦ • ❦

Life has its share of joys and laughter—but we also know
life's road is often very rough. Temptations assail us; people
disappoint us; illness and age weaken us; evil and injustice
overpower us. Life is hard—but God is good, and heaven is real.

BILLY GRAHAM

I t is so hard to imagine Billy Graham having regrets. It just does not seem to match up with our image of him. The ends do not meet somehow. Perception based squarely on years of observation left me little doubt this man was under the watch-care of our heavenly Father, and under His hand of protection. How could it be possible for a man of his caliber and stature to have any regrets at all?

Not so, said the man himself. Saturdays with Billy, albeit militantly confidential, bore witness to an unapologetic and openhearted—although rare—botheration with certain regrets. It became apparent rather quickly that this precious man thought little of himself when compared to the perfection of his Lord and Savior, Jesus Christ. Billy's deep and spiritual humility was, in and of itself, the very spark that ignited his regret.

The heart of his regret was his deeply felt conviction that he was not, in any way, worthy of any praise or recognition. No accolade was ever acceptable to him. Applause and recognition seemed to leave him bewildered at times. He often looked around to find who the people were applauding for. His face often reflected the shock he felt so genuinely when he realized people were appreciating his presence. Even in his later life, great effort had to be made to help him understand that he had something to say that others might need to hear.

> The heart of his regret was his deeply felt conviction that he was not, in any way, worthy of any praise or recognition.

His greatest regret was his perpetual inability to live up to the standards of God's holiness and righteousness. This meant that wealth and the things of life were as close to meaningless to him as one could possibly ever imagine. You could hear it every time he prayed. He would cry out to God for mercy and grace. Billy desperately desired for the Lord to hear him. He believed he needed help in every way. He regretted, deeply, his own sinfulness. When he did sin, his heart would break out of a deep sense of regret that he had committed an atrocity in the eyes of his Savior and Lord.

Perhaps one Saturday set the issue of regret in a proper framework. The evangelist was reminiscing about places he had visited. He sure loved to talk about those beaches and golf courses. The times with his family were cherished memories of fishing and walking all over the place—including the pathways that wound their way above the Graham homestead. One of his regrets was being away from home so much. It nagged at him. Any conversation about his travels seemed to make the circle back to an inner regret about being gone so long and so far. How deeply thankful he always was for his beloved Ruth. She was his rock and fortress. However, he regretted his absence from his family.

Mr. Graham was a very private man in many ways. As the years rolled by and our friendship deepened, the conversation became more intimate. This is what friends do when they share. I always felt he trusted me to hold what he said sacred, but some things came out in public, even when he least expected.

On a number of occasions, he brought up his lifetime of regret at having "betrayed" the trust of President Harry Truman by speaking to the press after having had a private conversation with the president. He believed it was one of the most embarrassing things of his life—even though he was young at the time. The picture of him kneeling on the front lawn of the White House with his close friends was a picture he believed served as a constant reminder to him about the humiliation he felt that day, and for years to come. "The thing about the Lord," he would say, "is that He does forgive—but He also has a way of giving a little reminder now and then!" By this time, he was able to crack that wonderful smile that would appear on his face and laugh, even at his own expense.

The public resurfacing of the Nixon tapes in 2005 caused us considerable discussion on a number of occasions. Perhaps two issues lay at the heart of his personal regret. One was the obvious fact the president was not the man Mr. Graham thought he was. He really loved and respected Mr. Nixon but seemed most perturbed that such unbecoming language could come from the mouth of this man. He deeply regretted he never knew this about Nixon. Furthermore, he regretted that, had he known, he could have counseled and helped the man understand the severity of his foul mouth. He believed very strongly that man confesses with his mouth and believes in his heart that Jesus Christ is Lord. His own hurting heart fueled Mr. Graham's regret for Richard Nixon.

More seriously, Mr. Graham regretted the incorrect information concerning his own voice on those tapes. On a call, President Nixon had been bemoaning the domination of the press and pointed much of the blame at the Jewish community. What sounded like the evangelist suggesting "the stranglehold" regarding pornography had to be broken

> He really loved and respected Mr. Nixon but seemed most perturbed that such unbecoming language could come from the mouth of this man.

was not, in the slightest way, a reference to the Jewish people, whom Mr. Graham loved deeply. Some people and newspapers jumped on the chance to suggest Mr. Graham was anti-Semitic. The context in which they rolled out Billy Graham's words was absolutely and completely false. He had a proven record and never spoke or suggested anything that would demean Jewish people.

One Saturday with Billy centered on this entire incident. He was shaken by it years after. It hurt him deeply. Not because he thought he may have said something he regretted—and now revealed by these tapes. No, he regretted being drawn into a controversy that, he knew, was avowedly false. He regretted having been in conversation with a man he thought he knew well. He regretted what he perceived to be his own lack of spiritual influence.

He said, "I feel as though the Lord has had me in the woodshed today." However, his regret did not leave him forlorn. Billy Graham saw this all through the eyes of a loving God. His desire to be completely obedient to the Lord Jesus kept him on his knees before the throne throughout his entire life. I recall the countless times we knelt before God and prayed for one another. Nearing the end, he could no longer kneel, but he always held my hand, and I prayed for guidance and wisdom for both of our lives.

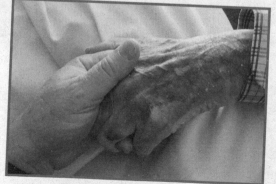

He could no longer kneel but held my hand when we prayed.

Mr. Graham preaching in Boise, Idaho, in 1982.

15

Billy's Mantle

❧ • ☙

> Your yearning for God must supersede all other desires. It
> must be like a gnawing hunger and a burning thirst.
> **BILLY GRAHAM**

All who knew Billy Graham were affected by his life and testimony. Who can measure this adequately? Surely, there are no words. No books can be written. No speeches made. What can we say except thank you to our God for His most generous and precious gift to our world?

Scores of people are now in heaven because they heard the truth coming from the lips of this one man. These saints come from every tribe and every nation of the world. Regardless of their ethnic group, all people are precious in God's sight. Mr. Graham told them all the same thing, "God loves you, and you, and you!" He told us all. He spoke straight from the heart. His heart. The heart of a servant of the living God. Thousands upon thousands of people, beginning with his own family, find themselves bearing a mantle of blessing. Many have no idea how they received it. Some have not stopped long enough to consider it.

Many somehow carry it. Some picked up this mantle by reading a book or an article about his message of the cross. Some just felt him coming through the pages of *Decision* magazine. Some were actually there. They remember well that crusade when Billy Graham looked up from his beloved Bible and said, "I'm going to ask you to come, no matter where you are seated. From way up there, to right down here, I am going to ask you to come!"

And they did.

Some met him at a press conference where he did not seem too interested in talking about himself, but rather about the reason he was in their city, state, or country: "God loves you," he said as though for the very first time every time. "Jesus belongs to the whole world!"

> "God loves you," he said as though for the very first time every time.

A mantle is a legacy. A legacy is the story of a person's life worth passing on. On Saturdays, Billy talked about this from time to time. He particularly loved studies in the life and times of some of the great prophets of God. He sure loved to go back to Moses. His meeting with God on Mount Sinai was the encounter that set the course of his life as God's deliverer. America's pastor derived much pleasure at the suggestion that Moses' "Sinai" encounter might be considered as his "Mordecai Ham" encounter!

As an aside, but very critical to his understanding of salvation, Billy certainly believed that conviction of sin, which leads to salvation, occurs when sinful man has an encounter with God the Holy Spirit. Ironically, however, while Moses always seemed to pop up in many a table-talk conversation, Aaron was often included in the discussion. Billy Graham loved to talk about Aaron. He constantly would talk about those incredible Aarons in his life and ministry. He loved them. In fact, had a fly been sitting on the lawn next to our conversation, the fly might well be led to believe that it was Aaron who was the most important figure in God's economy, and not Moses! Then, naturally, the discussion would go to Joshua. The evangelist believed implicitly that Joshua "wore" the mantle of Moses' life and legacy.

Many conversations centered around one of Mr. Graham's favorite verses of Scripture.

And so, it was, when they had crossed over, that Elijah said to Elisha, "Ask! What may I do for you, before I am taken away from you?" Elisha said, "Please let a double portion of your spirit be upon me." (2 Kings 2:9)

This is exactly what happened. Elijah's mantle "fell" on Elisha. His example became Elisha's example. Elijah's life was passed along to Elisha, and his light continued to shine.

Each person affected by the legacy of Billy Graham carries the mantle of his life in proportion to the time spent with him and the relationship experienced with him. Above all, each individual mantle is specifically identified by each person's calling according to the purpose of God.

A good example of this pertains to the question, "Who is the next Billy Graham?" The International Congress on World Evangelism was held in Lausanne, Switzerland, on July 16–24, 1974, for evangelists all over the world. There Mr. Graham was asked that question in front of twenty-three hundred evangelical leaders from 150 countries. His answer? "You all are," he said as he pointed at the crowd with the same hand that had pointed people to Jesus for decades. All believers are to share their faith in Christ. All believers are to be "fishers of men." Not just preachers. All who have called on the name of Jesus are responsible to share their faith in Jesus. Jesus said, "You shall receive power when the Holy Spirit has come upon you; and you shall be witnesses to Me in Jerusalem, and in all Judea and Samaria, and to the end of the earth" (Acts 1:8).

Perhaps Billy Graham's mantle can be partly understood in terms of five distinct areas of his life.

66 "Who is the next Billy Graham?"

First, in who he was. Mr. Graham was, foremost, a Christian man, saved and forgiven in and through the sacrifice of the Lord Jesus Christ. It was rare for this Christian man to talk with any person, or preach to any person, without every person knowing who he considered himself to be. There was no need to figure out, no guessing game, no mystery, and no silent adherence. Billy belonged to the Lord Jesus Christ. He was a Christian man.

Second, in what he did. From the day Billy surrendered his life to

Christ he was committed to serving Jesus Christ in every way and by whatever means. He was faithful to his calling and never strayed from a life of full obedience to Jesus Christ alone. What Billy did with his life was never up for much debate or discussion. He did what God wanted him to do, pure and simple. It was pure because it came from such a pure heart. He went about doing what the Lord told him to do because it mattered to him. God mattered. It was simple in that Billy Graham was uncomplicated about following the Lord's commands. Obviously, he and his team did everything with an uncommon standard of excellence. They did everything with the highest level of attention. It was done in the very best way possible, and no stone was left unturned in his personal preparation or the team's preparation. The hard part was all the work they needed to do. The simple part was just saying yes and getting on with it.

Third, in how he behaved. Some have correctly said, "Actions speak louder than words." Perhaps the mantle of blessing Billy Graham has passed on to all who would share the love of Christ found its beginning in his behavior. This dear man did not just preach about Christ. He walked the life of Christ. In another chapter, we gave attention to some of Billy's regrets. There it is. Even the slightest deviation in his behavior produced a spoken and visible response from the evangelist. It came from his heart. It just troubled him that he (in his eyes) had not acted right, or spoken to someone right, was abrupt, or had said something that may have caused someone to turn away from the Lord. This mantle was strong. The closer one gets to most people, the more one sees clay feet. Not so for this friend and pastor. The more I sat at the feet of this precious man, the more I saw the following verse true in his life: "having shod your feet with the preparation of the gospel of peace" (Ephesians 6:15).

Fourth, in whom he loved. Billy's love will always be an incredible mantle of blessing passed on for generations to come. One of the scribes in the New Testament asked Jesus which one of the commandments is first.

> Jesus answered him, "The first of all the commandments is: 'Hear, O Israel, the LORD our God, the LORD is one. And you shall love the LORD your God with all your heart, with all your soul, with all your mind, and with all your strength.' This is the first commandment. And the second, like it, is this: 'You shall love your neighbor as yourself.' There is no other commandment greater than these." (Mark 12:29–31)

Mr. Graham lived this out in word and in deed. Love God! Love others! Hardly a conversation with Billy Graham was completed without these spiritual beams shining brightly.

How much he loved God! It was an almost insatiable desire in his soul-spirit. It was a perpetual hunger and thirst after the righteousness of a loving God. It was an uncommon and relentless series of questions about God's Word—passages, verses, contexts, understandings, and applications. It presented an irony that could never be explained. It begged the question within me, "How could Billy Graham ask *me* to explain something about God and His Word?" Nevertheless, he wanted to know. He had to know because he loved the Lord with his whole heart.

His love for Jesus flowed like a relentless river into Billy's love for people. He really did love all people, because God loved all people. He passionately believed Jesus suffered on the cross, and God raised Him up in order that all who believed on His name would have forgiveness. This conviction lay at the heart of his passion to preach—even "just one more message" when his body began to feel the effects of his age.

Fifth, in where he went. Billy Graham's passion for the cause of Christ dismantled any and every wall of separation. No country was beyond consideration. No culture was off-limits to the team. He left out no church. He left no person behind. For Billy Graham, Jesus' command to "go into all the world" meant exactly what Jesus said (Mark 16:15). The message of the cross was the only barrier breaker. It was man's only hope. It was *my* hope!

When the Lord Jesus called Billy Graham home to heaven, many wondered about the mantle God had placed on his shoulders. One needs only to look at the evangelist's children and grandchildren. One needs only to consider the millions who were touched by his life and testimony. This great gift—the gift of the love of God in and through the Lord Jesus Christ—keeps on giving through every person who believes in His name.

16

Billy's Hope

❧ • ❧

I've become an old man now, and I've preached all
over the world. And the older I get, the more I cling
to the hope I started with many years ago.
BILLY GRAHAM

When my phone rang, my friend and brother in Christ, Franklin Graham, was on the line. "Don," he said after a few minutes of chitchat, "I want to ask you if you would help my father preach what may be his final message."

I could not imagine a higher honor. Mr. Graham's vast world was shrinking rapidly. With every passing month, his body became just a little bit more reluctant to get up and go. His wonderful voice cracked a little more, it seemed, every day. His hearing was not sharp. His eyes struggled to see as clearly as they once did.

But not his heart! No sir! The fire that burned for Jesus was undiminished. The voice that spoke, "God loves you" across planet Earth was still echoing those same words of hope. His firm conviction that Jesus Christ is "the way, the truth, and the life" resided in his soul-spirit like a rock-solid anchor (John 14:6). It did not seem to matter that his world was limited to his home. It made no difference that fewer people were able to come and visit with him. Oh, he loved them for sure. He talked about those who meant so much to him. He reminisced and recalled many fond encounters with many good friends.

Saturdays with Billy seemed like one long and grand conversation. All it took was the mention of a place or a country or a personality or an event, and his memory reached back. Many times, way back in the past. Long before I was even a thought. Long before we became close.

> His firm conviction that Jesus Christ is "the way, the truth, and the life" resided in his soul-spirit like a rock-solid anchor (John 14:6).

The day God called Billy Graham to preach the gospel, that was exactly what he did. He shared the hope of the cross because that was the passion of his life. It was the centerpiece on his mantelpiece. Everything was important to him, but few things really mattered to Billy more than sharing this real and living hope. This hope was evident in the way he lived, the places he went, how he spent his time, and the content of his conversation.

As the years rolled on by, and as his age advanced, his inability to preach became the subject of many of our conversations. He could not shake the desire to preach "just one more time." Of course he could not! This was the fabric of his being. This was the very reason he even existed. It was his call. This was his commitment to God. Moreover, everyone who knew him knew this too. His spirit was never more willing, but his flesh was extremely weak.

By the time Mr. Graham had reached his ninetieth birthday, he was genuinely encouraged by the way Franklin was continuing to lead the Billy Graham Evangelistic Association to be Christ-centered in every way. However, he was deeply concerned about the rapid decline of Christ-centered preaching and teaching among so many in America. He lamented the loss of focus on Jesus. He grieved the loss of conviction about the inerrancy of the Bible. "The Bible says" was not just Billy Graham's catchphrase. It came from his deep and abiding conviction concerning the real meaning of truth.

The long months he spent working on his book *Salvation* seemed to reignite the fire that burned so deep in his heart and soul. Each conversation seemed to find root in the essential theme of the book he was writing. I particularly recall two passages of Scripture that Mr. Graham wanted to discuss at depth. The first passage was 1 Peter 1:3–5:

> Blessed be the God and Father of our Lord Jesus Christ, who according to His abundant mercy has begotten us again to a living hope through the resurrection of Jesus Christ from the dead, to an inheritance incorruptible and undefiled and that does not fade away, reserved in heaven for you, who are kept by the power of God through faith for salvation ready to be revealed in the last time.

Billy Graham with the video crew for *My Hope.*

The second passage of Scripture was Revelation 1:1–3:

The Revelation of Jesus Christ, which God gave Him to show His servants—things which must shortly take place. And He sent and signified it by His angel to His servant John, who bore witness to the word of God, and to the testimony of Jesus Christ, to all things that he saw. Blessed is he who reads and those who hear the words of this prophecy, and keep those things which are written in it; for the time is near.

This was the central issue: Jesus Christ, our Lord and Savior! Jesus Christ, the Son of the living God! Jesus Christ, our living hope! Jesus

Saturdays with Billy

Christ, our salvation! The book he was working on focused on the essentials of our hope in Christ. The cross of Christ was central to this hope. Jesus came to earth, was born of a virgin in Bethlehem, died on a cruel Roman cross, was buried for our sin, and then was raised by the power of God. Jesus Christ is now ascended and is seated at the right hand of God and is making intercession for sinners. The death, burial, and resurrection of Jesus were fundamental to our hope in Christ through faith.

At Franklin's suggestion, Mr. Graham would share this message of hope from his own living room. Those months of taping were unforgettable, not only for me, but also for the entire crew of men and women who were amazing in the way they served together. From the very first day, it was evident Mr. Graham was continually being filled with the Holy Spirit. Arriving each day long before the appointed hour, Mr. Graham and I would go over some of the points he wanted to make as he prepared for the day, not without occasional humor! Especially when he turned to the lady doing his makeup and asked, "Why are you doing this to me when Don needs it far more than I do?" Point well taken, Mr. Graham.

The director positioned Mr. Graham facing the cameras and me. My responsibility was simply to prompt him from time to time. He was fully satisfied that the script we had were his words and from his heart. This was Billy Graham preaching, and preach he did.

Fatigue was, obviously, a real issue for Mr. Graham. He and I paused often and requested coffee for our breaks. During one break,

Don Wilton praying after explaining that so many people need to hear
the message of hope, especially from God's servant.

Mr. Graham leaned over to me and said, "Don, I just cannot do this anymore! I think we just need to stop the whole thing. I simply am exhausted and feel feeble and totally inadequate."

With my mind racing and a significant prayer in my heart, I asked Mr. Graham if he would consider stopping at that point but not canceling the entire project. The reason, I suggested, was that so many people needed to hear this message of hope, especially from God's servant.

The next suggestion came from Mr. Graham. "Don, could you just read one line to me at a time? I will simply just repeat the line."

What happened next was something none of us will ever forget.

Saturdays with Billy

I read the line, taken from Mr. Graham's exact words on the script. The evangelist began to repeat that line exactly. However, this time he did not pause or stop. For the next few minutes, it was as though the Holy Spirit rose up from the feet of God's peerless servant, journeying though his body, entering his eyes, and then speaking through his voice, mouth, and lips.

Sitting directly in front of Mr. Graham, I felt like I saw the stadiums of the world appear in Billy Graham's eyes. Mr. Graham was in his pulpit. He was in his parish. He was preaching the gospel. The people were there. He could see them in their lostness. He could see them in

Dr. Wilton speaking at Billy Graham's 95th birthday celebration at the Grove Park Inn in Asheville, North Carolina

their hopelessness. He could touch them. He was telling them about Jesus. He was inviting them to "come forward" and give their lives to Christ. He was preaching. He was preaching about *the cross*!

I froze in my seat. The television crew was vigilant behind the cameras for fear of losing the moment. His staff stood motionless in awe. We dared not breathe or blink for fear of missing this miracle unfold before our very eyes.

Then he stopped. The silence was beautiful. No one dared to interrupt the holy hush. God was in the house. The Holy Spirit had spoken through God's servant, Billy Graham.

As I sat there trying to wrap my mind around what had just happened, I remembered something that Brother Billy had often reiterated: "In great weakness, I would stand up to preach, and I would then sense a power coming upon me."[8]

After a long pause, all I knew to say was, "Would you like a cup of coffee, Brother Billy?"

My Hope America with Billy Graham: The Cross was watched by over 2.5 million viewers across the nation. In addition, it was aired on some fifty-three network affiliates, and more than ten million people viewed the program there. Thousands watched it around the world on YouTube as well as on the Billy Graham Evangelistic Association website. On a designated Sunday in November, Christians across the country invited people into their homes and churches for a special viewing of the program. Only the Lord knows how many people gave their hearts to Jesus. More than nine hundred people viewed *My*

Hope America at a special celebration of Mr. Graham's ninety-fifth birthday at the Omni Grove Park Inn in Asheville, North Carolina. Many guests were there, including men such as Rupert Murdoch, J. W. "Bill" Marriott, as well as the future president of the United States of America, Donald Trump, and his wife, Melania.

———— ❧ • ☙ ————

Billy Graham preached the gospel one more time in his lifetime, but his ministry continues today through TV, the internet, and crusades all over the world. Billy passed the mantle on to his family as well as every Christian who ever heard him preach. Today it is our responsibility to preach the message just one more time.

17

Billy's Convictions

❧ • ☙

Oh God, if You want me to preach, I will do it.
BILLY GRAHAM

Billy Graham was a man of deep and abiding conviction. Perhaps never a truer statement about him can be offered. It began with his person. The way his personhood offered itself was enough to leave anyone with little doubt as to the extent of this man's faith. Most who knew him recognized this about him. Even those who only met him on a limited number of occasions recognized a pureness of heart that he lived out in his daily life.

Obviously tall in stature, the evangelist carried himself with recognizable confidence. Mr. Graham was an imposing man. When he walked into a room, he offered a pause in his stride that left others wondering what he was about to say. Even the way he sat down on a chair and ate his food sent out a quality of persuasion. He had a way of looking straight ahead, for the most part, before turning his deep blue eyes on those who sat with him. His eyes would lock in, giving the speaker the feeling that whatever he was sharing with Mr. Graham had better be good. Then he would listen intently, giving full attention to those who were speaking to him.

He had a most striking Piedmont accent that seemed handcrafted by the very hills and mountains that cascaded down from behind the home before plunging over the picket fence and into the towns of Montreat and Black Mountain below. The familiarity of his voice immediately conjured up the messages he preached all around the world. People who did not really know him may have considered it best not to interrupt him. However, they soon discovered he was not menacing in the slightest. Their hesitation, perhaps, was based on his imposing stature and world-renowned reputation. It usually only took one or two moments in his presence for them to calm down.

As our friendship deepened, the back-and-forth of conversation took on a life of its own. Mr. Graham's deep convictions about his own lowly station in life produced, in and of themselves, a politeness felt by all who knew him. I must also say, however, there was seldom any misapprehension about what he needed done! Questioning his directives was not a consideration for those who were privileged to serve. They served him well because they trusted him completely.

Never one to elevate his own status or station in life, Mr. Graham frequently deflected conversations away from himself. His theological and spiritual beliefs governed much of his conversation. His deepest longing was to know God in all of His fullness. To the evangelist, any conversation that engaged his convictions was considered a priority. Especially when it came to the Lord Jesus Christ. Jesus, to him, was "the way, the truth, and the life." Period. This was not open to debate any more than his faith concerning the inerrancy of the Word of God. The Bible was and is absolutely true from cover to cover—every word! He believed the Holy Spirit is the very means by which a person is drawn into the heart of God, and that salvation is the direct result of the convicting power of the Holy Spirit.

Mr. Graham saw himself as an instrument in the hands of a holy and righteous God. His role was clearly outlined in the Bible. He believed salvation is only possible when a

Never one to elevate his own status or station in life, Mr. Graham frequently deflected conversations away from himself.

sinner repents before God, confesses to Jesus Christ alone, and then by faith accepts the finished work of Christ on the cross. He loved to discuss Ephesians 2:8–9: "By grace you have been saved through faith, and that not of yourselves, it is the gift of God, not of works, lest anyone should boast."

Billy Graham lamented the meteoric rise of "works" salvation, which he believed was responsible for so many people going to a Christless eternity. Jesus Christ was the only One who paid the full price for sin. He did this by going to the cross and taking on Himself the sin of man. He died, was buried, and God raised Him to life on the third day. "Preach Christ Jesus," he would often say to me. "Never preach another version of Jesus!" There is no other. As Paul said in 1 Corinthians 2:1–2, "I, brethren, when I came to you, did not come with excellence of speech or of wisdom declaring to you the testimony of God. For I determined not to know anything among you except Jesus Christ and Him crucified."

This Bible passage lay at the heart of Billy Graham's convictions. Nothing else mattered except Jesus. By nothing, he meant absolutely nothing—not money, not fame, not fortune. Nothing. Only Jesus. The question, then, was how Billy saw himself in the context of "only Jesus."

Here again, Mr. Graham drew on his conviction that God had called him to be an evangelist. His role was to travel the world and proclaim the gospel message, exclusively centered in the person and work of the Lord Jesus Christ. "Never take your call to preach the gospel lightly," he would advise. He often quoted Romans 10:13–15:

> For "whoever calls on the name of the LORD shall be saved." How then shall they call on Him in whom they have not believed? And how shall they believe in Him of whom they have not heard? And how shall they hear without a preacher? And how shall they preach unless they are sent? As it is written: "How beautiful are the feet of those who preach the gospel of peace, who bring glad tidings of good things!"

This passage was Mr. Graham's clarion call to do what God had called him to do. This was what drove him to be a man of prayer. He was convinced that he could not rise to the level of God's command to preach the gospel without the power of prayer. Therefore, he prayed and he prayed. Mr. Graham prayed in his closet privately. He prayed constantly with his beloved wife. He prayed publicly with his friends. He prayed earnestly with his team. He wrote about prayer. He taught prayer. He modeled prayer. He practiced prayer.

The spiritual surge he derived through prayer helped carry him to the farthest corners of the earth. Prayer was the very means that sustained him during his long absences from his family. Prayer preceded every message he preached and every sermon he prepared. He believed God not only heard his prayers but also answered his prayers. Billy Graham took Philippians 4:6–7 to heart: "Be anxious for nothing, but in everything by prayer and supplication, with thanksgiving, let your requests be made known to God; and the peace of God, which surpasses all understanding, will guard your hearts and minds through Christ Jesus."

For Mr. Graham, prayer was the vehicle given by God's love for us in and through the Lord Jesus Christ, enabling us to enter into a dialogue with God.

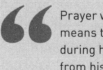

Prayer was the very means that sustained him during his long absences from his family.

"Supplication" was the manner with which we come before the Lord in prayer. For him, it was essential to be sincere and earnest in the making of petitions before the Lord. Prayer was, therefore, no light-hearted matter. Furthermore, Billy Graham considered prayer a great joy and privilege. However, it was never to be trifled with or treated in a manner that would not please the Lord.

The profundity of his theological convictions formed the core of the messages he preached across the world. Perhaps this was one of the greatest lessons Mr. Graham passed along to me personally. Early in our relationship, his sheer joy of discussing my preaching from the pulpit each Sunday, and on television throughout the week, became evident.

On one occasion, he took me for a walk on a pathway above and behind the house. He asked me what I was preaching on the next day. This was a common question. After I told him where I was in the Scriptures, he simply said, "Well then, Don, why don't you preach a little!" I soon realized this was not a suggestion, and so I began to preach a little. Quickly, Mr. Graham interrupted me and said, "Don't worry about me. Just look down toward the house and preach your text for tomorrow!" By now, I must admit I was somewhat anxious! Nevertheless, I began to preach the sermon (from my memory) to the trees. I could sense Mr. Graham somewhere behind me. Again, he stopped me and said something I will never forget.

"Preach like you actually believe what you are preaching!"

With that, I am certain the good folks way down in the town of Montreat might have heard me!

> "Preach like you actually believe what you are preaching!"
> ~ Billy Graham to Don Wilton

"Don," Mr. Graham said, "if you cannot preach to trees like you actually have deep convictions about the Word of God, why do you think God would want to actually put people in front of you to hear you?"

Saturdays with Billy

Ouch!

He went on to share with me how he, as a young preacher in Florida, would go out and preach to the tree stumps! What a man of conviction!

I believe that advice has helped me today as I preach. Little did I know, when Mr. Graham took me out to preach to the trees, that many years later I would preach to an empty church for many weeks due to a global pandemic! Praise the Lord for technology that allows more people to hear the gospel than we could ever fit into our church. When preaching to an empty church, I envision the faces of the people who are watching from all over the world on social media, the internet, television, and livestreaming. It amazes me how the Lord used Billy Graham to prepare me for a global crisis many years before it happened.

Billy Graham preaching to a crowd in Tampa, Florida, in 1979.

18

Billy's Church

❦ • ❧

No church is perfect, but don't let that discourage
you. Someone has said that if you ever find one that
is, it will stop being perfect the minute you join.
BILLY GRAHAM

A nd be sure to go to church Sunday!" Hardly a crusade anywhere
in the world closed without these final words of encouragement
from the evangelist.

The reason was simple and yet multifaceted. Billy Graham loved
the local, New Testament church. This was evident on my Saturdays
with Billy. Mr. Graham's usual question regarding my sermon for the
next day not only put the fear of the Lord in my heart, but I realized it carried more significance than at face value. Billy Graham did
not simply want to know about the content of the message, but rather
so much more. It had to do with this wonderful gathering of God's
people. It had to do with the real meaning of fellowship, encouragement, and growth—all so vital to every believer.

Mr. Graham felt somewhat deprived of all of this. Understandably so, too, considering his itinerant preaching. He was constantly on the move and had no place to just be and soak up the fellowship of God's people on a consistent basis. He mourned this fact. It hurt him deep down. He longed for intimacy with fellow Christians beyond the fame and grand expectations that accompanied his aura. From time to time, and much to my delight, he would insist on saying grace over our meals together because he felt that I was always expected to say the blessing because I was the preacher. How right he was!

The church was that seemingly untouchable place for Mr. Graham. It was one of the holes in his heart because he could not be part of it. Not that he regretted this fact or that he in any way bemoaned his inability to attend church, but he longed for this at the deepest level.

> " The church was that seemingly untouchable place for Mr. Graham. It was one of the holes in his heart because he could not be part of it.

The local church, he believed, was God's provision for all believers. By God's design, it was that special place where believers could gather and fill up their gas tanks for the journey that lay ahead. It was that place where understanding and equipping joined hands together through committed and trained pastors and shepherds of the flock of Christ. He needed that. On many occasions Mr. Graham opined that he might have handled situations and circumstances a little better or differently had he just been able to sit and listen to someone teach the truth of God's Word on a consistent basis.

Saturdays with Billy

Billy certainly had many wonderful pastors who meant so much to him around the world. Even on the home front, his long membership at the First Baptist Church of Dallas, Texas, was very dear to his heart. But he seldom was able to worship there or be part of those smaller gatherings and life groups. He longed for that connection.

Dr. W. A. Criswell, longtime Dallas pastor, was a dear friend to him. They shared many experiences together, and Mr. Graham valued his pastoral counsel. During one conversation about Dr. Criswell, I jumped on the bandwagon and began to extol his virtues. Mr. Graham interrupted the avalanche of praise and said, "Now, don't get carried away telling me how wonderful W. A. was to all who were blessed by him. He wasn't *that* wonderful—how could he be? He never was able to convince Ruth to become a Baptist!"

Her Presbyterian roots and his Baptist roots remained a constant source of conversation and joy, as well as much teasing and laughter.

Then an unexpected day came.

It was Saturday, and I invited my oldest son, Rob, to accompany me to visit Mr. Graham. I had no idea what was about to happen. Upon arrival, I made my way to the study, where more than the usual numbers of the staff had been summoned to gather. I realized something was up.

Mr. Graham took the floor and began to share with his staff. "What I want you to know today is that I have asked you all to come here to hear what I have decided to do. Dr. Wilton knows nothing about this, and I have never discussed this specific subject with him

> Her Presbyterian roots and his Baptist roots remained a constant source of conversation and joy, as well as much teasing and laughter.

before. Dr. Wilton has not only become my very close friend but he is also my pastor. I want to formally ask him if he would consider having me as a full member of his church and congregation."

The sweetness of that moment will never fade.

I took the matter to my congregation the next Sunday morning. One could hardly describe the joy or the honor as members and friends of the First Baptist Church, Spartanburg, South Carolina, stood to their feet in every worship service to express their heartfelt and humble joy in the receiving of Dr. Billy Graham as a member of the church.

That week, Sunday with Billy was a certainty! Right after the conclusion of the last worship service, I jumped into my motorcar and roared up I-26 and I-40 to see my friend (and fellow church member) and have lunch with him.

As I walked through the kitchen door with my usual, "Hello, Brother Billy!" I quickly added, "Would you like to hear the good news or the bad news first?"

He looked up with a twinkle in his eye and a smile on his lips as if to say, "Would it make any difference, knowing you?"

"Well," I began, "the good news is you are officially a member of First Baptist Church in Spartanburg!"

"What's the bad news?" he asked.

"The bad news is that it passed by one vote! You barely made it, Brother Billy, but in our church, the pastor has the deciding vote, like the Senate in Washington. So don't worry; I have your back on this!" Of course I was kidding him, but he loved it! He loved the fact that he was part of a local church of believers. He loved the fact that he could talk and counsel with his pastor. He loved the whole idea of being part of something Jesus had made so clear when He spoke to Peter at Caesarea Philippi and said, "On this rock I will build My church, and the gates of Hades shall not prevail against it" (Matthew 16:18).

What he said next was profound. He believed that when Jesus talked about His church, He was referring to every believer. Essentially this was because we are the temple of the Holy Spirit, who dwells in us (1 Corinthians 6:19). Furthermore, the evangelist strongly urged every believer to be fully engaged in going to church and being the church. He spoke often of his own personal struggle of "rightly dividing the word of truth" on his own (2 Timothy 2:15). He felt he needed his pastor and his church fellowship.

As difficult as it may seem to comprehend, Saturdays with Billy were frequently punctuated with Mr. Graham's questions to me as his pastor. He valued this at the highest level because he understood God's divine order. He understood the call of God from the perspective of his own life and calling. Regardless, Billy Graham believed the highest calling to serve the Lord was that of the pastor. He held pastors in the highest esteem. He held the church in the highest esteem. He held God's people in the highest esteem.

"Be sure to go to church Sunday" was not just a quip. Like a burning coal, the evangelist believed it was imperative for him to preach the gospel and call for salvation. This fire burned most brightly in him. Nevertheless, it was incomplete if he did not insist that these same people be in church. Without the church, their burn would fizzle. They would be like the proverbial coal, standing alone without the fire. This passion for the local, Bible-believing church was present in most everything the evangelist did.

> "Be sure to go to church Sunday" was not just a quip.

Way back in his early years, support for the local church became part of the "Modesto Manifesto," which he, Cliff Barrows, Bev Shea, and Grady Wilson had formulated. The manifesto's third point highlighted the team's commitment to partner with the work and ministry of the local church. Mr. Graham believed this was not only biblical but also ethical in that it showed their unequivocal support for pastors and ministers of the gospel.

Saturdays with Billy supported this in so many ways. He constantly affirmed me as a brother and friend, but also as a pastor—his pastor. It is extremely difficult to explain, but it was as though he considered me "higher up" than him! Try to figure this one out. It was as though God would speak to me, and my job was to pass this along to Mr. Graham. I realize this does not make any sense at all. I, in fact, hesitated to write about this for fear of sounding self-serving. However, this was Billy Graham. Humble. Loving. Personally undeserving. Void of grandeur.

Saturdays with Billy

Abandoned. He believed in God's order. Jesus established His church. Period. No place in the Bible did He say anything about any other!

Billy Graham was "in on God" all the way. No shortcuts. No half measures.

Mr. Graham preaching in Spokane, Washington, in 1982.

19

Billy's Friday

Life is short; none of us knows how long we have. Live
each day as if it were your last, for someday it will be.

BILLY GRAHAM

On Friday, February 18, 2018, I drove my motorcar up I-26 from Spartanburg, South Carolina. My schedule dictated that I visit Mr. Graham on Friday as opposed to the normal Saturday visit. I had no idea this would be my last visit with this most precious man of God. I knew the time was coming. He talked about it often, but it never crossed my mind that this was Billy's last Friday.

As usual, I approached the intersection of I-40 and I-26 outside Asheville, North Carolina, and my vehicle routinely knew which way to turn. We had done this many times together. Mostly on Saturdays, for sure.

Saturdays were great days to visit with Mr. Graham. For one, the two of us could watch some great golf or other sports. For another, it was a good day for a busy pastor to be out of town. For another, the evangelist was preparing to carry out his calling, as I was.

In the earlier days there were speeches, prospective meetings, and visits with people, and, of course, the crusades—the Billy Graham Crusade in Tampa, Florida, in 1998; Nashville, Tennessee, in 2000; Louisville, Kentucky, in 2001; Dallas, Texas, in 2002; Oklahoma City, Oklahoma, in 2003; and San Diego, California, in 2003. The calendar was full. In fact, we often mused that it seemed like every person in the world who came to visit the United States of America wanted to meet with Billy Graham. Let alone all the people of the United States whom Mr. Graham loved so well. His final crusade was at Flushing Meadows–Corona Park in New York City in 2005. Mr. Graham was eighty-six at the time, and his body was failing him. He had preached to more than 210 million people around the world.

He knew it back then in New York. Speaking to a packed-out news conference, he said, "I've been asked so many times lately, do I fear death. No, I look forward to death with great anticipation. I am looking forward to seeing God face-to-face. And that could happen any day!"

I remember that wonderful interview on CNN's *Larry King Live* in 1994. He said the same thing to his friend Larry, and to all of America.

It happened just as Mr. Graham thought it would happen. He grew older. As the years passed, his world closed around him. Saturdays with Billy became any day with Billy. His schedule was opening more by the day, and my privilege was to be his

> "I look forward to death with great anticipation. I am looking forward to seeing God face-to-face."
> ~ Billy Graham

Saturdays with Billy

pastor and friend. He was always gracious, insisting that he knew "you can't possibly come now, but when you are able!" Besides, he would remind me, "You have the single greatest honor God could give to any man—to be the pastor of such a wonderful congregation of people."

It was a very cold day. Both my motorcar and I were used to the sudden drop in temperature from Spartanburg, South Carolina, to Montreat, North Carolina. How grateful I was my motorcar had four-wheel drive!

I backed into my usual parking spot outside the kitchen door entrance and noticed no other vehicles except for the staff. This was common at this stage of his life. Outside of his family and the members of his staff, it was not possible for others to visit.

As I walked through the door, I shouted out my usual, "Hello, Brother Billy—it's me!" I greeted the staff and headed through the kitchen, which held memories of laughter, conversation, questions, answers, and, of course, great meals. I took a quick turn into the sitting room and then another quick right toward the bathroom. There on the wall hung a magnificent photograph, a gift from Charles Stanley—a fellow preacher of the gospel and dear friend to Mr. Graham over the years. This was one of Dr. Stanley's inspiring works of photography. Mr. Graham loved the rainbow that always provoked many conversations about the promises of God.

"Tell me how you tap into the promises of God," I asked him during one of our times together. He opened his Bible and began to read:

I will lift up my eyes to the hills—from whence comes my help? My help comes from the LORD, who made heaven and earth. He will not allow your foot to be moved; He who keeps you will not slumber. Behold, He who keeps Israel shall neither slumber nor sleep. The LORD is your keeper; the LORD is your shade at your right hand. The sun shall not strike you by day, nor the moon by night. The LORD shall preserve you from all evil; He shall preserve your soul. The LORD shall preserve your going out and your coming in from this time forth, and even forevermore. (Psalm 121:1–8)

How many times he came back to talk about the promises of God! I remembered he and Ruth quoted the late William Carey at the opening of the Billy Graham Training Center at The Cove: "The future is as bright as the promises of God."

I walked all the way down the hallway, glancing at the picture of him reclining in the lap of the love of his life, Ruth. The sitting room teemed with memories the family will cherish all their lives. I could see a glimpse of Christmases past when, at his request, I would invite the ministry team of his church to come and surround Mr. Graham with the joy of Jesus' birth.

> I could see a glimpse of Christmases past when, at his request, I would invite the ministry team of his church to come and surround Mr. Graham with the joy of Jesus' birth.

Those were truly happy times. Perhaps the best was sitting between Billy

Saturdays with Billy

Graham and Bev Shea on the couch. The team led in the singing of Christmas carols but quickly disintegrated as Mr. Bev would lean over to Mr. Graham with a big smile on his face and say something like, "Come on, Billy, sing out!" Only Mr. Bev could do this! In addition, listening to Bev sing was as if the angels were there doing it again!

As I reminisced, the house became more vivid and intense than I ever remembered. I turned left and walked down the hallway to the study. My mind flooded with memories of conversations, events, and time spent together. As I look back, it is obvious this was a precious gift from God. Each picture preached a message about the life and testimony of just one man. My mind was trying to capture every detail, as if it were the last time I would ever be there. Now I understand.

I could see Mr. Graham in his chair as usual. My friend and brother in Christ. "Hello, Brother Billy," I said, knowing there would be little response. He was resting peacefully. His head was leaning gently forward as he napped. I walked around to his left side, where I always sat. I talked intermittently just in case he could hear me. "How's the day been, Brother Billy? Looks like you didn't eat your lunch today. Wow, Brother Billy—the traffic today was unusually heavy. You should have seen the backup as I passed the Biltmore. I think there was a wreck, judging by the police vehicles all over the place! By the way, Brother Billy, don't forget to remind me to read you a story about a man who gave his life to Jesus when you were preaching in England years ago! . . . You feel like watching a bit of TV today? . . . I haven't forgotten what you told me about the things you did to keep yourself focused on Jesus when you preached. . . . How about some good ribs from Twelve Bones?"

He continued to sleep. Of course, I saw him move a little and even try to lift his head, but it just seemed like he was not up to the effort.

For some hours, we sat together. Just the two of us. I read several passages of Scripture to him. Then, as I was accustomed to doing, I reached out and said, "I have to go, Brother Billy." In so doing, I took my right arm and again placed it around his shoulders. He was wearing his favorite-color shirt and sweater—blue. He also had on his blue jeans. For extra warmth, he had a light blanket draped over him. Reaching across him with my left hand, I gently pulled the blanket up to his neck, sensing he may have been a little cold.

I began to pray to the Lord Jesus for both of us. Suddenly, Mr. Graham just slightly leaned his head to the left and laid it on the side of my neck. The words I was saying to Jesus were intermingled with tears.

Then he did something I will cherish for the rest of my life. He slowly and shakenly shifted his right hand and slid it ever so gently to touch my hand. With his hand cupped over mine, we sat for what seemed an eternity.

Eventually I kissed his cheek as I always did and left to make the trip down the mountain, unknowingly for the very last time.

20

Billy's Heaven

❧ • ☙

I would not change places with the wealthiest and most influential
person in the world. I would rather be a child of the King, a joint
heir with Christ, a member of the royal family of heaven.

BILLY GRAHAM

This time it was not Saturday. This time it was not with Billy.

On Sunday evening, after preaching, my wife and I jumped into my motorcar for the two-and-a-half-hour drive to Boone, North Carolina. How could anyone not really love this quaint town? There are spectacular panoramic views of mountains, clear streams of water, and hundreds of walking trails to enjoy as well as wonderful people to meet. This is not the real reason I love Boone.

Boone is the home of Samaritan's Purse. Franklin Graham, son of Billy and Ruth Graham, is the president of Samaritan's Purse as well as the president of the Billy Graham Evangelistic Association. What wonderful organizations! Samaritan's Purse mobilizes an army of people who give of themselves around the world in disaster relief, medical ministries, and just about anything and everything where people are afflicted. Most importantly, all is done in the name of the Lord Jesus Christ.

The honor of an invitation to lead their spiritual week in Bible study each day was deeply humbling.

Tuesday, February 21, 2018, arrived. As I recall, it was a beautiful day in Boone. The air was very cool but crisp and vibrant as my wife, Karyn, and I arrived at the Furman Building for another great time of fellowship with so many wonderful people around the Word of God.

I parked my motorcar in the special lot, close to the entrance of Furman, ready to go at 9:00 a.m. After I spoke, I was going to have lunch with Billy Graham.

As the scores of people flooded into that magnificent facility, I could sense the Lord speaking to my heart. I felt, deep down, that God was there again. His Spirit was evident.

I opened God's Word, and everyone dialed in.

Suddenly, several people simply stood to their feet and walked toward the entrance. A strange, very real sense of "something is going on but I have no clue what it could be" came over me. I continued to preach the Word of God but realized I was losing my audience. By now, people had begun to whisper to one another. My mind began to go in different directions. Then I noticed several of the leaders abruptly leaving. I must admit I thought about Franklin. He had been with us the day before but had left for Dallas, Texas. Had something happened to him?

I looked down to the front table, where my wife was sitting, for a clue. She was holding a piece of paper up so I could see it. On it, Karyn had written:

"Mr. Graham has just gone to be with Jesus!"

It was about 8:30 a.m. I looked to my left into the face of Ron Wilcox, COO of Samaritan's Purse, as he approached the lectern. As I stepped back, he simply announced, "Dr. Billy Graham has passed away into the presence of the Lord Jesus."

Bryan Willis, the director of special events at Samaritan's Purse, was there to take hold of me. As he led me off the stage, my head was spinning in some ways. I had spent last

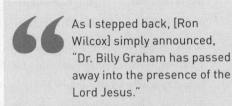

As I stepped back, [Ron Wilcox] simply announced, "Dr. Billy Graham has passed away into the presence of the Lord Jesus."

Friday with Billy. We had held hands together. We had prayed and asked the Lord Jesus to bless His servant Billy Graham.

As I climbed into my motorcar, the thought came to me. I thought I was going to have lunch with Billy Graham, but God decided otherwise. It was time for Him to bring Billy home.

As I drove down the mountain to the Billy Graham Training Center at The Cove, my mind was full of thoughts and memories. Thoughts about God's angels came to mind. How much Mr. Graham loved to talk about angels. He would often talk about the one that gave those shepherds the shock of their lives. "Just one angel," he would remind me. God's special ambassador, sent to come and bring "good tidings of great joy which will be to all people" (Luke 2:10). "This clearly established the meaning of good news," Mr. Graham would say with conviction. He loved to talk about the multitude of the "heavenly host" rushing together, praising God and saying, "Glory to God in the highest, and on earth peace, goodwill toward men" (Luke 2:13–14).

One time I preached a series on angels, and I asked the evangelist to assist in the gathering of my thoughts. He was so humble. He told me he had written a book about angels but knew little about them. The conversation continued time after time. He talked of the angels who appeared at the empty tomb. They said to the women, "Why do you seek the living among the dead? He is not here, but is risen! Remember how He spoke to you when He was still in Galilee, saying, 'The Son of Man must be delivered into the hands of sinful men, and be crucified, and the third day rise again'" (Luke 24:5–7).

The angels he talked about so often had given him a royal escort into the presence of almighty God. This was Billy's heaven. He was home.

> " The angels he talked about so often had given him a royal escort into the presence of almighty God. This was Billy's heaven. He was home.

Mr. Graham remembered those words from Luke when thinking about his beloved Ruth, especially after her death. Dreams became part of his life in his later years. Oftentimes we would sit together and he would

A portrait of Billy's beloved Ruth at the foot of his bed.

tell me detailed accounts of dreams he was having. Many centered on Ruth.

One of these involved a most beautiful picture. There was a magnificent landscape in his dream. The hillsides were adorned in splendor. "Myriads of flowers wafted in the breeze, and trees lined themselves up everywhere," he said. Billy Graham found himself walking toward this majestic scene, and while he was doing so, he thought he remembered seeing Ruth high up on the mountainside, picking flowers and singing. He began to run toward her but could never get there. She never turned to look at him. All of a sudden, there was a huge river between them. He shouted and called to her, but she

Billy's Heaven

did not respond. Abruptly, he woke up! He was back in his room—alone. All he could do was look over the top of his bed to the beautiful picture of his beloved Ruth.

On another occasion, we were having tea on the front porch of the house as the dogs were playing around. Every so often I would get up and throw another stick for them to chase. Sam wagged his tail a lot, and China joined in. Cat was not at all interested in the game. One look at Cat left the distinct impression that life was boring!

I noticed Mr. Graham preoccupied for the longest while. Initially I thought he might not be feeling too well on that day. Perhaps he was just being quiet. Then I noticed he kept turning to his right. It was a slow turn, perhaps more of a sideways glance. I followed his gaze up to a small window. This was no ordinary window; inside was the kitchen sink. The ultimate workplace. It was the high-action zone of the happiest room in the house—if one were to measure all the family activities that ebbed and flowed from the sink of the kitchen.

"I can see Ruth," the longing husband whispered. "I can see her standing there . . ."

Judging from the sweet tone of his voice and the gentleness of his expression, I hesitated to say anything. I did not want to interrupt his longing. I did not want to bring him back to the reality that the love of his life was waiting for him to join her at the feast table of the King.

> He often was heard saying, "The moment we take our last breath on earth, we take our first in heaven."

Saturdays with Billy

"The most thrilling thing about heaven is that Jesus Christ will be there. I will see Him face-to-face. Jesus Christ will meet us at the end of life's journey." He believed this with all of his heart. The absolute certainty of life after death was a constant topic of conversation on Saturdays with Billy. He could not help himself talking about the joy of heaven. An unknown bystander would have no doubt that Mr. Graham believed everything the Bible said about heaven was literally true. He certainly did. No questions here. He understood the active ingredient of faith. He knew there was so much we, as human beings, simply will never fully grasp, especially about how we are raised from the dead. However, for Billy it was not complicated. First, he just took God at His word. He trusted the Lord in every way. He often reminded me that my role as a preacher was never to try and get people to understand the great mysteries of God, but rather, to preach the Word of God with conviction and in the power of the Holy Spirit. He often was heard saying, "The moment we take our last breath on earth, we take our first in heaven."

Nevertheless, this did not stop him from missing Ruth. He pined for her—but not in a "lack of faith" kind of way. He just missed her. He missed her voice, her face, her presence, and her love.

Billy's heaven began long before February 21, 2018. It began when he accepted Jesus as his personal Savior and Lord. He always seemed to have heaven on his mind. He knew he was simply passing through this life—heaven is his eternal home.

21

Billy's Name

The work has been God's and not man's. I want no credit
or glory. I want the Lord Jesus to have it all.
BILLY GRAHAM

I was startled from a deep sleep as the phone at my bedside rang very early on the morning of February 22, 2018. "Good morning, Don. Are you coming to breakfast?" It was Franklin Graham. I realized we were at the Billy Graham Training Center at The Cove.

Billy Graham was in heaven.

As I tried to shake the sleep from my eyes, I found myself thinking about a question Mr. Graham had asked me several years earlier. It was on a Saturday, and we were enjoying the day just strolling around the front of the house. We enjoyed a delicious lunch as we sat together and had a long chat.

"I want to talk with you about my funeral," Mr. Graham said.

This was a common topic of our conversations. I knew Franklin had thought through all of the details, and Mr. Graham had asked me to "preach his funeral message." At that early time, it was all I knew. I did not really want to talk about Mr. Graham leaving us. I could not imagine our world without him. I did not want to go there, really. To me, he was such a powerful witness for Christ. It seemed everyone knew whose ambassador Billy Graham was. They knew. Powerful people knew. Rich and poor people knew. Politicians knew. Both Republicans and Democrats—and Independents too! They all knew. Even the queen of England knew. People around the world knew that Jesus would be at the center of the evangelist's conversations. If you hear Billy Graham talk or preach, you hear about Jesus. If you sit down with Billy Graham, it is as if Jesus is there with you. If you discuss the world, you discuss Jesus. If you look for solutions to problems, Billy will lead you to look to Jesus for the answer.

The "bomb" Mr. Graham dropped on me while sitting out there that day made perfect sense, but it all came together as the sun began to rise on that crisp and clear Wednesday morning at The Cove.

"Hello, brother," I said to Franklin as I walked into the dining room at The Cove. It was still dark outside, and it appeared we were alone. I wanted to reach out and give him a big embrace. I understood the enormity of the responsibility that rested on his shoulders. I could see the resemblance to his father in Franklin's eyes as we sat there talking. Very soon Will Graham joined us at the table as we began to finalize the plans for the days to come.

It was just one day since God had dispatched His angels to gently pick up Billy Graham and give him a royal escort into the presence of Jesus. In my mind's eye, I could see the journey. I could only imagine the multitude of angels as they escorted the magnificent chariot, adorned with gold plating. The wheels sparkled with precious stones as time and space were absorbed into God's galactic sovereign sphere of eternal endlessness. As the chariot arrived at heaven's gate, Billy heard a familiar voice. "It's about time you arrived, Billy!" There she was—Billy's beloved Ruth. I could imagine the two of them walking through the gates of heaven only to be greeted by the sound of a crusade choir so massive in scope, no one could ever overexaggerate the numbers of people. Billy and Ruth stopped to listen and watch. There, leading the choir must have been Cliff Barrows and singing a solo, Bev Shea. I even imagined the words to his song had changed, and he was singing, "I now have Jesus, He is everything to me!" The angel assigned to lead them to the throne of God leaned over and said, "Billy, these are the hundreds—no, thousands, no, thousands upon thousands of people from all over the world who gave their hearts and lives to the Lord Jesus as a result of your faithful witness!"

When Billy asked me to preach at his funeral, he made a particular request: "Don, I have asked you to do this because I trust you. I want you to know that I do not want my name mentioned at my funeral."

As the chariot arrived at heaven's gate, Billy heard a familiar voice. "It's about time you arrived Billy!" There she was— Billy's beloved Ruth.

My whole life seemed to float by, and I sat and tried to digest what Mr. Graham was asking me to do. I understood where this was coming from instantly. This was Billy Graham. His humility was the hallmark of his life and testimony. His only desire was to serve the Lord Jesus. It would seem Billy Graham just did not matter.

This point is well made when one visits the Billy Graham Library in Charlotte, North Carolina. It is a living testimony to the Lord Jesus Christ. Thousands of people each year draw near to the heart of God as they meander through one testimony after another. Every detailed aspect of the library, from the devoted and engaging staff to the detail of the ministry and message of Billy Graham—all centered on the person of the Lord Jesus Christ.

The moment Mr. Graham first watched the video plans for the exhibits and galleries is well documented. "Too much Billy Graham," he said to Bill Pauls, who continues to be a faithful man to the ministry. It happened again with *My Hope America*. After months of filming and months of praying, the time came for an initial look at the final product. Mr. Graham did tell me, as well as a few others, that he was "not entirely happy with it." If he had his way, there would be "no Billy." Just Jesus!

> The moment Mr. Graham first watched the video plans for the exhibits and galleries is well documented. "Too much Billy Graham," he said.

But at his funeral? Thousands (his permitted term) may (his permitted term) be watching. How does one preach Billy Graham's funeral without ever mentioning Billy Graham?

With my mind racing, I

Saturdays with Billy

suggested we talk a little about Moses. We did. Just consider Moses, I asked of the evangelist. We both agreed it was incredible the way the Lord used Moses to deliver the children of Israel from the hand of Pharaoh.

We talked about God's redemptive plan. We talked about the Lord Jesus Christ being the only means by which man can be saved. Finally, I added the capturing statement: "Brother Billy, don't you think it is incredible that the Lord would use a man like Moses and add the story into His Word for all to read?" He agreed that it was an amazing story.

I was pleading with the Lord to open Mr. Graham's heart. We switched passages at this point and dove into Jesus telling us about the rich man and Lazarus in Luke 16. Jesus said this, I reminded Mr. Graham. He never would have said anything false. Jesus had no need to concoct a story in order to convince us of the absolute certainty of life after death. The picture Jesus gave was clear. Once in hell, the rich man was crying out for mercy. Hell was an eternal certainty. When he realized how final death was and when he realized he was never going back to earth again, his only thoughts were for his five brothers who were still alive on earth. He now was passionately concerned they would give their hearts and lives to Jesus. He began to beg Abraham "'that you would send him [Lazarus] to my father's house, for I have five brothers, that he may testify to them, lest they also come to this place of torment.' Abraham said to him, 'They have Moses and the prophets; let them hear them'" (Luke 16:27–29). Again, I explained that God used Moses in incredible ways, and Jesus mentioned his name in the Bible long after Moses died!

"Okay, I get it," Mr. Graham interrupted. He looked over at me and took what seemed like the longest time. Then he said, "Okay, Don. You can mention my name. But only just a little bit!"

I thought I might have detected a smile slowly creeping across his face. However, on closer reflection, there was no smile. There was also no anger at all. And most certainly there was no trace of any disdain or unhappiness with the way I had gone about trying to convince Billy Graham just how important he was, in fact, to all the Lord had done over the many years through his life and ministry.

The look on his face was contemplative. It was earnestly serious. It was somewhat resigned. Had his face been able to tell us what was in his heart, it might have said, "Well, go ahead if you need to. I understand the need of people to have someone to be the topic of their conversation. But everything I am and everything I have ever done has only been about the Lord Jesus."

He must increase, but I must decrease! (John 3:30).

22

Billy's Boast

❧ • ☙

Sin was conquered on the cross. Christ's death is the
foundation of hope, the promise of triumph!
BILLY GRAHAM

Franklin asked me to accompany him and his oldest son to the funeral home. As we drove from The Cove to the funeral home, the vibrant testimony of Billy Graham seemed to radiate from the very blue sky above our heads. Throngs of people were already gathering on the streets. The drive back to The Cove with Mr. Graham's body was even more poignant and deeply touching. I noticed a man there among the many who had gathered. He was standing at attention with his hand placed over his heart in a gesture of thankfulness. A little farther down the road, another person with a sign in hand caught my attention. The sign read, "God bless you, Billy Graham." It looked like it had been hand-drawn from the heart of just one more person who was deeply touched by this man.

The procession turned off Interstate 40 to enter the Billy Graham Training Center at The Cove. People were beginning to assemble in the main building. In addition to the Graham family, the men and women who had served Mr. Graham for years joined many close friends. These included the nursing staff as well as many who had served well. Many came and stood near his casket, positioned on the stage in the auditorium. Franklin handed me a Bible. I opened it and underlined Galatians 6:14: "But God forbid that I should boast, except in the cross of our Lord Jesus Christ, by whom the world has been crucified to me, and I to the world."

This verse was Billy's Graham's boast. As a young teenager, he gave his life to Christ. When God called him to be an evangelist, he devoted his life to Christ. When he preached across the world, he preached about Jesus Christ. When he met with people, he talked about Jesus Christ. When he prayed, he always prayed in and through the name of Jesus Christ. When he talked about his funeral, he only wanted to glorify Jesus Christ. When he told people of all nations and tribes and customs and religions how to inherit eternal life, he told them the only One was the Lord Jesus Christ.

In at least two key places in his home, Mr. Graham had posted Galatians 6:14. When he sat at his favorite table in the kitchen, he was reminding himself. "God forbid that I should boast, except in the cross of our Lord Jesus Christ."

> " But God forbid that I should boast, except in the cross of our Lord Jesus Christ, by whom the world has been crucified to me, and I to the world.
> ~ Galatians 6:14

Saturdays with Billy

Cliff Barrows, Billy Graham, and George "Bev" Shea singing "This Little Light of Mine."

This was the room where, most often, he would meet with others. This was the room where he would enjoy fellowship around the kitchen table. He loved to sit in this room and look out over the front lawn.

The other place he posted this verse of Scripture was in his bedroom quarters. This was his retreat. This was where he could go to be alone. This was where he could really be far from the adoring crowds. This was where his boast really mattered.

Whether talking on the phone, eating his meal, conversing with his friends, preparing in his study, or relaxing on his bed, Billy Graham consistently made his boast about the Lord Jesus Christ.

As his casket lay on the platform of the auditorium at The Cove, people were flooded with thoughts and memories. They had watched him walk and had heard him preach. Close friends had sat with him at the tables of the world and had met for private times of planning and preparation for crusades and other events. They all knew about his boast. They all anticipated the Lord Jesus Christ would manifest His glory at the funeral of Billy Graham.

As the family gathered to pray, the presence and power of God were evident. After a family time of prayer, Mr. Graham's body was taken out of The Cove to the awaiting hearse. During this time, precious servants of the Lord Jesus formed an honor guard of love. Many had tears rolling down their cheeks, and many felt the deep-down tug of love so deep for a man so faithful and so true to his Lord and Savior. Just as Mr. Graham's body was placed in the hearse, the singing of "This Little Light of Mine" was heard rising above the honored silence. While here on earth, Billy sang "This Little Light of Mine" many times with his two brothers in Christ, Cliff Barrows and Bev Shea. Would the light of Billy Graham's life ever be put out? A resounding no still rings out as the legacy of Billy Graham lives on and portrays the love of Christ to all people.

As the procession began that memorable journey to Charlotte, it was immediately evident the light of Mr. Graham's testimony was about to shine brighter, perhaps, than ever.

People lined the highways and intersections. They stood shoulder to shoulder on bridge overpasses. They carried banners and American flags. Police officers, military personnel, and firefighters

David Bruce (Billy Graham's executive assistant) and Don Wilton escorting
Billy Graham's casket into the Rotunda just after the procedural knock.

joined thousands of others as they honored and thanked God for this
man of God.

The next day thousands came to the Billy Graham Library to pay
their respects and to say thank you to the Lord Jesus Christ. As he lay in
the old homestead, President George W. Bush, former First Lady Laura
Bush, and President Bill Clinton came to pay their respects. Busloads
of people arrived, including most of the staff from Samaritan's Purse
in Boone, North Carolina. As people filed by the place where Mr.
Graham lay, they shared words with the family, and each, it would
seem, boasted of the Lord Jesus Christ.

The following day the city of Charlotte stood still as the procession
made its way to the Charlotte airport. It seemed the airplanes stood

aside on the runway as Mr. Graham's body was gently lifted into the airplane that would carry God's servant to Washington, DC.

Crossing the Potomac River, the procession slowly made its way past the White House and on toward the Capitol of the United States of America. In the lead car, I leaned forward and whispered to the chief agent, "Thank you, sir, on behalf of Mr. Graham and his family, for all you are doing for him today."

"An act of Congress," he said. "Highest honor in the land." Billy Graham, this most humble servant of the Lord Jesus Christ, was only the fourth private citizen to lie in honor in the Capitol Rotunda.

"Ready, step!" the commander of the full military honor guard shouted out. With magnificent precision, Mr. Graham's body was slow-stepped all the way up the flight of stairs leading to the inner chamber. They halted at the interior door; a procedural knock signaled it was time. Mr. Graham was greeted by the president and the vice president of the United States, the first and second ladies, members of the president's cabinet, members of the Supreme Court of the United States, members of both the Senate and the House of Representatives, the Speaker of the House, and the Senate Majority leader. Every speaker, including President Donald Trump, pointed to the life and testimony of the man Billy Graham.

Then it happened. The sound of Billy's "Just as I Am" softly filled the Rotunda. Michael W. Smith began to play and sing the same words sung by thousands across the world.

Don Wilton and David Bruce (second row) escorting Mr. Graham's casket down the Rotunda steps.

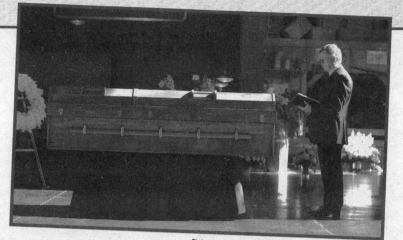

Dr. Wilton reading Galatians 6:14 from Billy Graham's Bible at the end of Mr. Graham's casket.

> Just as I am, without one plea
> But that Thy blood was shed for me
> And that Thou bid'st me come to Thee
> O Lamb of God, I come.[9]

This was the seat of the most powerful nation in the world. They were there. Men and women of great prominence. People from every state in the United States of America. President Trump himself. Republicans and Democrats. All watching. All listening. All seeing.

No, this was not about greatness. This was not about fame. This was not about wealth and power. This was not about achievement. It was simply about one man and his God. It was about the one thing that matters. It was about Jesus Christ, the Savior of the world.

"Ready, step," the commander of the military honor guard shouted

Saturdays with Billy

again as Mr. Graham's body was methodically escorted down the steps of the Capitol Rotunda and into the waiting hearse.

———— ❧ • ☙ ————

On March 2, 2018, Billy Graham lay in the main entrance of the Billy Graham Library as final preparations for his funeral service were being made. The family was all gathered.

Moments before the president of the United States, Donald J. Trump, and the First Lady Melania Trump accompanied by the vice president of the United States, Mike Pence, and the Second Lady, Karen Pence, entered the room to greet the family, I quietly moved over and stopped directly in front of Mr. Graham's casket. My back was toward the huge cross that is the single stamp of why the library even exists.

"Hello, Brother Billy," I tried to say quietly to my dear friend as I opened the same Bible that had stood in front of his casket at The Cove. "I wish I could just tell you one more time how much I love you. You're in heaven now, Brother Billy, with Ruth—just like we talked about."

I experienced a flood of emotions as I stood there saying goodbye to my friend. My personal loss in a human sense was very deep. I had lost a very dear friend and mentor. It was an undue privilege to sit at the feet of Billy Graham all these years, to learn from him, to be mentored by him, and to be prayed for by him. I do not know why he loved me like he did, but I am eternally grateful to the Lord to have been touched by his life.

As I stood at the end of his casket that day, I looked down, and my Bible was opened to Galatians 6:14. "But God forbid that I should boast except in the cross of our Lord Jesus Christ, by whom the world has been crucified to me, and I to the world."

As I bowed my head, the sun seemed to burst through the window, shadowing the cross and beginning to make its way forward to touch the top end of Billy Graham's casket. It was as if the Lord were saying, "It is all about what Jesus did on the cross."

This was Billy's final boast.

23

Billy's Secret

———— ❧ • ❧ ————

Someday you will read or hear that Billy Graham is dead. Don't you believe a word of it! I shall be more alive than I am now. I will just have changed addresses. I will have gone into the presence of God.

BILLY GRAHAM

How does one explain Billy Graham? What was the key to his life? Mr. Graham's vibrant testimony for the Lord Jesus Christ will burn brightly for generations to come. Scholars, students, and the people of God will continue to write about him, discuss him, and offer opinions about the secret to this man's amazing life for generations.

The answer to Billy's secret was clearly displayed as the world stopped to watch and listen as Billy Graham was being laid to rest. Some two thousand people from over fifty countries met under a simple tent to say goodbye. Millions around the world livestreamed not only his funeral service, but also as family and close friends gathered in the Billy Graham Library's Prayer Garden for a burial service to say their final goodbyes.

It was noon on March 2, 2018.

As the family of pallbearers began to escort Mr. Graham's body from the library to the massive tent, the presence of the Lord Jesus Christ was powerfully evident. Billy's ultimate secret was there. His name is Jesus. However, He is no secret. All those in attendance knew Jesus is no secret. He is the One who saved Billy Graham. He is the One who forgave Billy Graham of all of his sin. He is the One who called Billy Graham to serve Him all the days of his life. He is the One who placed His hand on Billy Graham and set him apart to be an evangelist to the world. He is the One who strengthened him by the might and power of His Holy Spirit. He is the One who spoke through him by His Holy Spirit and His Word.

It was time to say goodbye. The evangelist's own words were alive with each step taken by the pallbearers. "With all my heart I want to leave you with truth." Those eleven words, spoken at the core of *My Hope America* with Billy Graham, served not only to unleash the key to life and death but to encompass the message Mr. Graham had preached for eight decades all around the world. It was all about the Lord Jesus Christ. Salvation and the forgiveness of sins, found only through the death, burial, and resurrection of Jesus Christ, the Son of the living God. "All that I have been able to do, I owe to Jesus Christ," he said. God had found in Billy Graham a man He could trust with this precious gospel. He was a man after the heart of God.

The tent overflowed with a who's who of men and women from every sector of life. The presence of the president of the United States of America, the vice president, and their wives was indicative of the honor afforded this one man.

In row upon row were seated people who had come just to say thanks. Scores of them had significant ministries that reverberated around the world. They were part of a spiritual army, engaged in a spiritual battlefield. Each person came with individual frames of reference, many with hearts that beat for the Lord Jesus Christ. They helped explain Billy Graham. There they were—all people for whom Christ died. Many came from affluent and influential backgrounds in their own right. However, most gathered in the same parking lot, boarded the same crowded bus, drove the same highway, and sat together in the same tent. These men and women were all there with the same purpose.

Mr. Graham's secret lay deeply embedded in the kind of man he was. He was the same to all people. It mattered not where they came from or what they owned or possessed. It mattered not the color of their skin or the language they spoke. It mattered not their gender or creed. Mr. Graham reached out to them as equals. No, indeed, as a servant of the most high God. Every person who knew him felt his servant's heart. It was strange but true. He met with presidents, prime ministers, kings, and queens. He had deep friendships with famous people around the world, and all loved him and sought his godly counsel. To each and all he shared the love of God in Christ Jesus. He never wavered or hesitated. "For I am not ashamed of the gospel of Christ, for it is the power of God to salvation for everyone who believes" (Romans 1:16).

Mr. Graham's secret lay deeply embedded in the kind of man he was. He was the same to all people.

He was quoted as saying, "I never go to see important people, or anyone else, without the deep realization that I am, first and foremost, an ambassador of the King of kings. I am always thinking of ways I can share Christ."[10]

Billy Graham was never motivated by rancor, anger, or condemnation, but only by the love of God, without compromise. He never lowered the bar of expectation. He embraced human individuality while recognizing that Jesus Christ died for all people. Various factions criticized Mr. Graham for associating with people some might think unacceptable. For example, he went to the Soviet Union at the height of the Cold War. Many warned that people would misinterpret his visit as fraternizing with the enemy, but he went nonetheless because God had put it in his heart to do so.

While there, at a conference in Moscow, a member of the politburo got up and roundly criticized him. Mr. Graham did not respond to the criticism when his turn came to speak. Instead, he shared the message of Christ. He spoke with a heart of tenderness and warmth. For years after that event, he preached behind the Iron Curtain and in many Soviet satellite countries. Countless numbers of communists heard the gospel, and scores came to accept Jesus Christ as Lord and Savior.

Cliff Barrows often recalled a profound memory he had with Mr. Graham and the team. They had just completed one of their crusades in London, England. Many people had stepped forward making decisions for the Lord Jesus Christ. Cliff and Bev Shea found themselves celebrating in their hotel room one evening when they noticed

Mr. Graham was sitting rather quietly by himself and was not participating in the celebration. They said something like, "Billy, wasn't that fantastic? Wasn't that incredible?" He looked up and simply said, "Only God gets the glory, boys; only God gets the glory."

Billy Graham's funeral was the powerful testimony of what God had done through this one man. The eighty-two-minute service seemed to be one magnificent, heartfelt invitation to follow the Lord Jesus Christ. It was all about the Lord Jesus. The impact of Mr. Graham for Jesus glowed through the powerful and moving tributes and mes-sages given by his five children. Those who brought messages in song pointed everyone to the throne of God. When Franklin stepped to the same pulpit from which his father had delivered the good news for decades and to people around the world, he pointed people to Jesus—just as his father had always done.

"Only God gets the glory, boys; only God gets the glory."

~ Billy Graham

As the procession moved slowly back to the library, the bagpipes sounded the tune: "Amazing grace, how sweet the sound that saved a wretch like me. I once was lost, but now I am found; was blind but now I see."[11] The life and testimony of Billy Graham were on full display.

The family and close friends, shortly thereafter, gathered in the Billy Graham Library's Prayer Garden. There he would join his beloved Ruth. It was there we were reminded of Galatians 6:14: "But God forbid that I should boast except in the cross of our Lord Jesus Christ . . ."

This passage of Scripture was not simply posted on the walls of Billy Graham's home. The living Word was speaking from the grave. The message was clear: Mr. Graham's body was there. His casket was there. But not God's peerless servant. He had been raised from the dead. He was very much alive in Christ. "But if the Spirit of Him who raised Jesus from the dead dwells in you, He who raised Christ from the dead will also give life to your mortal bodies through His Spirit who dwells in you" (Romans 8:11).

> To God be the glory, great things He has done!
> So loved He the world that He gave us His Son
> Who yielded His life an atonement for sin
> And opened the life gate that all may go in.
> Praise the Lord, praise the Lord, let the earth hear His voice
> Praise the Lord, praise the Lord, let the people rejoice
> O come to the Father through Jesus the Son
> And give Him the glory, great things He has done.[12]

Out of the many truths I learned through my relationship with Billy Graham, there is one embedded in my heart that has changed my life and ministry. I remember clearly the many times he said to me, "Don, don't ever share the gospel without giving people a chance to give their hearts to Jesus."

So I would be remiss if I did not give you the opportunity to give your heart to the Lord Jesus Christ now. God loves you! There is no other way of salvation except through the cross of Jesus Christ. The only way to the Father is through His Son, Jesus. Jesus Christ will save you, forgive you of your sins, and make you a new person. Come to Christ! Accept Him today. Admit you are a sinner and that you need forgiveness. Put your trust in Him and He will forgive you and guarantee your eternity in heaven. Call the number on the following page and talk with someone 24/7. Jesus will give you hope and change your life forever.

Has *Saturdays with Billy* touched your life?

WOULD YOU LIKE
TO GIVE YOUR
Heart to Jesus?

Contact us by calling today:

866-899-WORD (9673)

24-Hour Live Confidential Prayer Line

Acknowledgments

——— ✿ • ✿ ———

O n one occasion a rather important person was visiting Mr. Graham in his home. During their conversation he turned to the evangelist and, while looking at me, asked, "Dr. Graham, how did you and this man get to develop such a close friendship and personal relationship?" After a very typical pause, Mr. Graham looked up at him and said, "God!"

I first want to thank the Lord Jesus Christ for allowing me to sit at the feet of one of God's peerless servants.

I cannot thank my wife, Karyn, enough. The sacrifices she made were a hallmark of our lifelong partnership in ministry. She loved me, supported me, encouraged me, joined me, and sent me off Saturday by Saturday, and then some, with unity in love.

My deepest gratitude and thanks to Dr. David Bruce. He, too, stood alongside Mr. Graham while encouraging and partnering with me and the entire team in every way. David also read the manuscript, joining in our unapologetic commitment to fact-check and make certain that memories of the mind and joys of the heart are, nonetheless, a true and living reflection of the life and legacy of Billy Graham's testimony for the Lord Jesus Christ.

Heartfelt thanks is also given in abundance to Mrs. Jimmie Davis for her untiring devotion in the assembling of my many years of information and its application in writing and submission.

I am so grateful to Jack Countryman for bringing this all out of me and for encouraging me to put my recollections in writing.

I cannot overstate how much I loved seeing such an amazing staff most weeks I visited the Montreat home. Each one served Mr. Graham with such devotion and tenderness as unto the Lord Jesus. They became my friends, and I cherish each one so much. What a team.

My fellowship and deep appreciation for Franklin and the Graham family continues as the love of God in Christ Jesus is shared around the world.

Notes

— ❧ • ❧ —

1. "The Cross—Billy Graham's Message to America," Billy Graham Evangelistic Association, November 7, 2013.

2. Billy Graham, *Just as I Am: The Autobiography of Billy Graham* (New York: HarperCollins, 1997), 697.

3. Laura Bailey, "The Night Billy Graham Was Born Again," Billy Graham Evangelistic Association, November 6, 2017, https://billygraham.org/story/the-night-billy-graham-was-born-again/.

4. Charles Haddon Spurgeon, *Lectures to My Students: A Selection from Addresses Delivered to the Students of Pastors' College, Metropolitan Tabernacle* (New York: Robert Carter and Brothers, 1889), paraphrased.

5. Laura Hillenbrand, *Unbroken* (New York: Random House, 2010), 375.

6. Charlotte Elliott, "Just as I Am," 1835, public domain.

7. Jerri Menges, "A Humble Start," *Decision* magazine, commemorative ed., 53, https://decisionmagazine.com/humble-start/.

8. *Decision* magazine, commemorative ed., "Billy Graham 1918–2018," 25.

9. Charlotte Elliott, "Just as I Am."

10. *Decision* magazine, commemorative ed., "Billy Graham 1918–2018," 67.

11. John Newton, "Amazing Grace," 1772, public domain.

12. Fanny Crosby, "To God Be the Glory," 1875, public domain.

About the Author

D on Wilton has been the senior pastor of the First Baptist Church of Spartanburg, South Carolina, for over twenty-seven years. He is the founder and president of *The Encouraging Word*, reaching people in all fifty states and internationally through television, radio, and the internet. He has authored many books, including *Totally Secure, The Absolute Certainty of Life After Death*, and *When God Prayed*. A native of South Africa, Dr. Wilton is a highly sought-after Bible expositor and is a frequent speaker for the Billy Graham Evangelistic Association, The Cove, Samaritan's Purse, and universities and seminaries around the world. Don and his wife, Karyn, have three grown children, who serve the Lord in ministry. They are the proud "Chief" and "Duckie" for eight grandchildren.

KNOW FOR SURE WHERE YOU WILL SPEND ETERNITY

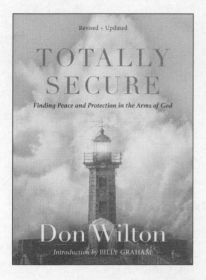

Outside of salvation, I do not believe there is a more serious question than this: "How do I know for sure that my salvation is totally secure?" Your salvation is not dependent on your emotions. Never gauge your salvation based on the roller coaster of emotions in life. Total security comes from the heart of God, not the feelings of man.

....

WHAT IS THE MOST HOPEFUL WORD IN HISTORY?

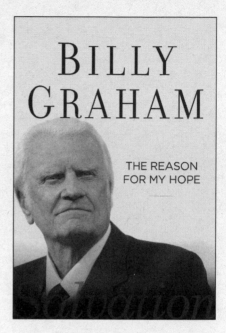

BILLY GRAHAM

THE REASON FOR MY HOPE

For Billy Graham, that word is *salvation*.

   Salvation is what we all long for, when we are lost or in danger or have made a mess of our lives. And salvation belongs to us, when we reach out for the only One who can rescue us—Jesus.

The Reason for My Hope: Salvation
is available wherever books are sold.

God's Word
overflows with hope

Billy Graham touched the lives of countless people with the good news of Jesus Christ. Share that gift of hope with one of his best-loved messages, *Hope for Each Day*, available in a beautiful, deluxe leathersoft cover. This book of 365 daily devotions will encourage your soul as you revel in the hope of Jesus.

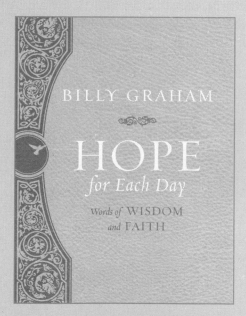

Hope for Each Day
is available wherever books are sold.